African Intellectuals
and Decolonization

This series of publications on Africa, Latin America, Southeast Asia, and Global and Comparative Studies is designed to present significant research, translation, and opinion to area specialists and to a wide community of persons interested in world affairs. The editor seeks manuscripts of quality on any subject and can usually make a decision regarding publication within three months of receipt of the original work. Production methods generally permit a work to appear within one year of acceptance. The editor works closely with authors to produce a high-quality book. The series appears in a paperback format and is distributed worldwide. For more information, contact the executive editor at Ohio University Press, 19 Circle Drive, The Ridges, Athens, Ohio 45701.

Executive editor: Gillian Berchowitz
AREA CONSULTANTS
Africa: Gillian Berchowitz '
Latin America: Brad Jokisch, Patrick Barr-Melej, and Rafael Obregon
Southeast Asia: William H. Frederick

The Ohio University Research in International Studies series is published for the Center for International Studies by Ohio University Press. The views expressed in individual volumes are those of the authors and should not be considered to represent the policies or beliefs of the Center for International Studies, Ohio University Press, or Ohio University.

African Intellectuals and Decolonization

Edited by

Nicholas M. Creary

Ohio University Research in International Studies
Africa Series No. 90
Ohio University Press
Athens

Ohio University Press, Athens, Ohio 45701
ohioswallow.com
© 2012 by Ohio University Press
All rights reserved

Printed in the United States of America
Ohio University Press books are printed on acid-free paper.∞ ™

20 19 18 17 16 15 14 13 12   5 4 3 2 1

Library of Congress Cataloging-in-Publication Data

African intellectuals and decolonization / edited by Nicholas M. Creary.
    p. cm. — (Ohio University Research in international studies. Africa series ; no. 90)
  Includes bibliographical references and index.
  ISBN 978-0-89680-283-4 (pb : alk. paper)
  1. Africa—Intellectual life—20th century. 2. Africa—Intellectual life—21st century. 3.
Postcolonialism—Africa. 4. African literature—History and criticism. 5. Africa—In mass
media. I. Creary, Nicholas M. II. Series: Research in international studies. Africa series ;
no. 90.
  DT30.5.A3634 2012
  306.096—dc23   2011043454

This book is dedicated to all those for whom the struggle continues.

A luta continua mas vitoria é certa!

Pamberi na Chimurenga!

Contents

Introduction
Nicholas M. Creary

Introduction
Janet B. Hess
1

PART I: REPRESENTATION AND RETROSPECTION

We Need a Mau Mau in Mississippi:
Malcolm X's Political Lessons for Today
George Hartley
15

Nkrumah/Lumumba: Representations of Masculinity
Janet B. Hess
27

Trauma and Narrativity in Adichie's *Half of a Yellow Sun*:
Privileging Indigenous Knowledge in Writing the Biafran War
Marlene De La Cruz-Guzmán
37

PART II: DECOLONIZING PUBLIC SPHERES: CONFLICTS AND NEGOTIATIONS

The Emergent Self in South African Black
Consciousness Literary and Discourse
T. Spreelin MacDonald
69

The Public Life of Reason: Orchestrating Debate in
Postapartheid South Africa
Lesley Cowling and Carolyn Hamilton
83

Setting the Agenda for Decolonizing African Media Systems
Ebenezer Adebisi Olawuyi
102

The African Renaissance and Discourse Ownership:
Challenging Debilitating Discourses on Africa
Steve Odero Ouma
117

PART III: DECOLONIZING KNOWLEDGE: INTELLECTUAL
IMPERATIVES AND EPISTEMIC DIALOGUES

Decolonization and the Practice of Philosophy
Tsenay Serequeberhan
137

Beyond Gendercentric Models: Restoring Motherhood to Yoruba
Discourses of Art and Aesthetics
Oyèrónké̩é̩ Oyě̩wùmí
160

Contributors
177

Index
181

Introduction

Nicholas M. Creary

In his 1952 study, *Peau Noire, Masques Blancs*, Frantz Fanon point-edly asked: "Was my freedom not given to me then in order to build the world of the *You?*"[1] Asking this question on the eve of much of Africa's independence from European colonial occupation, Fanon displayed his typical prescience, foreseeing a nominally postcolonial Africa in which the continent would remain largely subjugated within a neocolonial world order. Moreover, Fanon foresaw a neocolonial world in which the process to liberation would be ongoing long after Africa's formal independence from European colonialism. Cape Verdean/Guinean nationalist leader Amílcar Cabral summed up this idea in the Portuguese language slogan "A luta continua" (The struggle continues).

Sixty years later, Africans continue to struggle to "decolonize the mind," that is, "to seize back their creative initiative in history through a real control of all the means of communal self-definition in time and space."[2] With regard to the production of knowledge of Africa and its representation, the incompleteness of the decolonization struggle is evident in the fact that Africa today remains widely associated with chaos, illness, and disorder—a range of colonial stereotypes that say more about the seer (the West) than the seen (Africa). That is, Africa remains largely known as the Other of a colonial, Western "*You.*"[3] As such, Africa is cast as a sociopolitical morass, a dead weight upon an outside (read white and Western) world presumably burdened with Africa's lack of development. This prevalent (mis)conception is nothing if not a latter-day invocation of the idea of "the white man's burden," so central in providing moral-evolutionary trappings to the brute violence of Europe's military conquest and colonial occupation of Africa, and enduringly instrumental in contemporary geopolitics.

To recognize the weight of this tremendously powerful association of Africa with inferiority upon intellectual work is to address the fact that, as Tsenay Serequeberhan argues herein, "behind the many and varied perspectives that constitute the philosophical tradition of the West, one finds the singular view—a core grounding axiom—that European modernity is, properly speaking, isomorphic with the humanity of the human per se." Thus, if Europe is the epitome of humanity in this dispensation, Africa is conceptually its *in*human counterpart. Or, put another way, the term "Black Human" is an oxymoron.[4]

Decolonizing the mind is thus the dual task of first, placing African discourses at the center of scholarship on Africa; and second, of dislocating African humanity from this human-inhuman binary. Africa cannot escape its subjugation within modernity simply by attempting to climb up through "development," as development does not disperse the antiblackness and anti-Africanness of Western modernity. As Emmanuel Eze pointedly observed: "We do not . . . have enough reasons to expect that once everyone is rich and educated, antiblack racism will disappear."[5] Although these days few contemporary scholars producing Western narrative discourses on Africa would refer to Africans as "primitive," current discourses frequently oppose Western "modernity" with "traditional" African cultures or practices—where "traditional" is a more acceptable euphemism for "primitive." In short, the binary opposition of a primitive or traditional Africa to a modern or enlightened West continues to pervade academic discourses, contemporary journalistic accounts of Africa and its peoples, and the perspectives of international development and aid organizations.

Thus, the challenge for African and non-African scholars alike is to establish the substantial and valid fact of African humanity, in all its diversity, and to enable the representation of Africa beyond its historical role as the foil to Western humanity. And so the quest for African subjectivity continues.

We take up this challenge in this volume, as the mandate within intellectual work, to continue to strive for the decolonization of the academy and its production of knowledge of Africa. Indeed, in the spirit of Fanon, Ngũgĩ wa Thiong'o, Cabral, Lewis Gordon, and other revolutionary thinkers, we follow Oyèrónkéẹ́ Oyěwùmí's dicta that

> the foundations of African thought cannot rest on Western
> intellectual traditions that have as one of their enduring fea-

tures the projection of Africans as Other and our consequent domination. . . . As long as the "ancestor worship" of academic practice is not questioned, scholars in African Studies are bound to produce scholarship that does not focus primarily on Africa—for those "ancestors" not only were non-Africans but were hostile to African interests. The foundational questions of research in many disciplines are generated in the West.[6]

In this spirit, we present a collection of essays that address the struggle to decolonize African knowledge and the roles that African and Africanist intellectuals play in this broader struggle.

In an effort to encourage the development of greater African knowledge and more accurate knowledge of Africa, the essays in this collection call on African scholars and scholars of Africa to formulate and apply intellectual theories and categories based on the concrete experiences of African historical agents. Presuming an equality of subjective voices within the academy, that is, if scholars can no longer privilege Western perspectives and practices over "non-Western" ones, then African voices have a right to be heard within intellectual discourses and a responsibility to represent themselves within intellectual discourses. Consequently, they must develop distinctively and explicitly African categories of intellectual inquiry. *Subaltern Studies* was a South Asian effort to that end. Thus, African scholars and scholars of Africa need to take advantage of academic and intellectual spaces opened by postmodern, postcolonial, and cultural studies theorists to rationalize African intellectual developments as explicitly African reflections upon the specific experiences of African historical agents. This is vital because African historical agents have made and continue to make their own histories; these histories do not portray Africans only as "primitive" conquered subjects, resisters, and/or collaborators.

Curiously, African philosophers and Africanist theorists and scholars have not inquired how Africans, in their own respective languages and systems of thought, conceptualized and expressed their individual understandings of the human "subject" and how each person relates to the broader cultural group. In a South African context, for example, would it be possible to explicate "human subjectivity" in terms of *ubuntu*, or the idea that "I am because we are"; that is, that one's human identity (or subjectivity) is radically bound to one's existence as part of a larger group? Or further still, is it possible to explicate *ubuntu* in its own right as a humanistic or philosophical concept? Even though some African philosophers such as Mogobe B. Ramose have made preliminary attempts to do so, the fact that others, including V. Y. Mudimbe, do not consider "African traditional [*sic*] systems of thought" as either African philosophy, or science, or "general intellectual configuration," begs the question.[7]

Moreover, the decolonization of Africa within fields of knowledge (epistemology), and especially the roles of intellectuals within this process, has been a central, if unresolved, question within this strain of anticolonial discourse. Consider, for instance, Aimé Césaire's excoriation of intellectuals within his seminal text, *Discourse on Colonialism*, for their roles in maintaining systems of oppression rooted in colonialist capitalism:

> Therefore, comrade, you will hold as enemies—loftily, lucidly, consistently—not only sadistic governors and greedy bankers, not only prefects who torture and colonists who flog, not only corrupt, check-licking politicians and subservient judges, but likewise and for the same reason, venomous journalists, goitrous academics, wreathed in dollars and stupidity, ethnographers who go in for metaphysics, presumptuous Belgian theologians, chattering intellectuals born stinking out of the thigh of Nietzsche, the paternalists, the embracers, the corrupters, the back-slappers, the lovers of exoticism, the dividers, the agrarian sociologists . . . and in general, all those who, performing their functions in the sordid division of labor for the defense of Western bourgeois society, try in diverse ways and by infamous diversions to split up the forces of Progress—even if it means denying the very possibility of Progress—all of them tools of capitalism, all of them, openly or secretly, supporters of plundering colonialism, all of them responsible, all hateful, all slave-traders, all henceforth answerable for the violence of revolutionary action. . . .
>
> And do not seek to know whether personally these gentlemen are in good or bad faith, whether personally they have good or bad intentions. Whether personally—that is, in the private conscience of Peter or Paul—they are or are not colonialists, because the essential thing is that their highly problematical subjective good faith is entirely irrelevant to the

objective social implications of the evil work they perform as
watchdogs of colonialism.[8]

Thus, intellectuals—African and Africanist alike—have significant roles to play in decolonizing the knowledge of Africa that the
academy, the media, and the arts produce.

Sixty years after Césaire leveled his critique, scholarship on Africa in North America and Europe has advanced significantly:
African intellectuals have taken up positions at some of the most pres-
tigious centers of research and education in the world, and frequently
have their works published by internationally recognized journals
and presses. African Studies centers and programs have proliferated
across university campuses throughout North America and Europe.
And yet, in many ways, these scholars, centers, and programs are
marginalized in their institutions. Frequently an African or Africanist scholar is the only person in her or his department (or institution) with any significant or specialized knowledge of the continent
and spends more time teaching general surveys instead of courses in
her or his areas of expertise, or conducting research, while colleagues
who specialize in American or European Studies are privileged to
offer more, and more specialized, courses in their areas of expertise.
Compare, for example, the number of Americanists or Europeanists
(classical, medieval, or modern) in a history department versus the
number of historians who teach African, Asian, or Latin American
histories, and the number and nature of the courses taught by each respective group. The scholars of the so-called "non-Western world"—
including historians of Africa—frequently comprise the minority of
the departments that teach about the majority of the world.

In the United States, scholars of Africa are often housed in "Africana" departments or programs that are principally staffed by specialists in African American or African diaspora (read "Afro-Caribbean")
studies, and are thus token intellectual representatives of the African
continent. Or the positions to which they have been hired will require
them to teach African American topics in addition to their fields of
expertise in African Studies. Institutionally, very few departments are
dedicated to African Studies (e.g., the Department of African Studies at Howard University in Washington, D.C.; or the Department
of African Languages and Literatures at the University of Wiscon-
sin Madison), and interdisciplinary programs in African Studies

frequently remain underfunded and understaffed, oftentimes having to share faculty lines with disciplinary departments. Or worse, the scholar is based in a disciplinary department and must volunteer her or his time and efforts to the African Studies program over and above departmental requirements for scholarship, teaching, and service. Thus, African and Africanist scholars are frequently hamstrung in their efforts to establish African subjectivity and combat the barrage of distorted and distorting images of Africa produced for popular consumption by various media in Europe and North America.

Sadly, African scholars who remain at institutions of higher education in the African continent face even greater challenges resulting from the ongoing neocolonial exploitation of African states. Economic structural-adjustment programs imposed on African states by the World Bank and International Monetary Fund (IMF) have resulted in African governments' drastically reducing funding for tertiary education. Consequently, African scholars spend more time teaching instead of conducting research, and frequently teaching overcrowded classes in dilapidated infrastructures with outdated technologies. Furthermore, many African scholars and intellectuals, such as Ngũgĩ and Ken Saro-Wiwa, who criticize their governments are sent to prison or into exile. Thus, conditions in African universities contribute to the "brain drain" of African intellectuals to Europe and North America, which is yet another facet of the neocolonial exploitation of African (intellectual) resources for the benefit of the West at Africa's expense.

In his many speeches and writings, Amílcar Cabral frequently reminded his audiences that "the struggle continues" (A luta continua), or that political independence was merely "the end of the beginning."[9] Colonialism was not a single moment or process.[10] Rather, it was series of multiple, overlapping processes of attempted domination that were simultaneously mutually reinforcing and disintegrative. Just as Africans chose from a variety of options to respond to colonial processes, including physical resistance (armed and nonviolent), organized and/or spontaneous rebellion or strike, negotiation, or collaboration with and support of various elements of colonial policies (e.g., African Christianities), the actions of colonialists—both in African territories and in European metropoles—often subverted colonial processes and inadvertently supported nationalist aims, for example, by teaching Africans literacy and numeracy in European languages. While their objective may have been to develop a Europeanized petty bureaucracy of African clerks who could help make colonialism cost-effective for the metropoles, one of the unintended consequences was to give emergent African nationalists powerful tools for communication and organization.

Similarly, decolonization must necessarily be a series of overlapping processes that were neither uniform in objectives, beyond expulsion of the colonizers, nor uniform in the tactics to be used to achieve those objectives. The essays in this collection interrogate the contributions of African, diasporic, and Africanist intellectuals to the struggle to decolonize the academy as part of the broader project to constitute and liberate African humanity and subjectivity.

This book is motivated by two beliefs: first, that Africa's decolonization is an ongoing process of struggle across a range of fronts; and second, that intellectuals—African and non-African alike—have significant roles to play in the processes of decolonization. We offer a collection of essays that address the central questions: How can intellectual work realize Africa in a manner that embodies value? What is the role of intellectual work in relation to contemporary Africa? What is the state of the struggle to decolonize African knowledges?

The significant contribution of this volume is to move the discussion of decolonization in Africa, whether as a single moment, a single process, or a series of processes, to the postcolonial period, and hopefully to begin a post-neocolonial phase in the academy. All of the essays address topics and themes present in African states and societies since those states achieved putative political independence. The essays in this collection thus not only address the enduring intellectual legacies of European colonialism in Africa, but also provide scholarly tools to assist more broadly in the ongoing processes of decolonizing the academy and the African continent.

We begin with the issues of representation and retrospection. The first section offers three essays that question the ways in which Africa's decolonization is commonly portrayed as a completed and failed (Hess; Hartley) or totalizing (De La Cruz-Guzmán) event, rather than an ongoing process of intellectual and epistemological contestation in African and (more broadly) Africana contexts. This sets the stage for deeper reflections on the process of decolonizing knowledge of Africa and the roles of intellectuals in this process in the rest of the volume.

The second section, "Decolonizing Public Spheres: Conflicts and Negotiations," presents different perspectives on the struggle to decolonize African publics. These different views draw out salient points of tension, such as the competing roles of intellectuals and governments, self-determination versus liberal nonracialism, and media reform.

In the final section of this volume, "Decolonizing Knowledge: Intellectual Imperatives and Epistemic Dialogues," essays by Serequeberhan and Oyěwùmí examine the fundamental questions of epistemic decolonization and/or the decolonization of knowledge, especially by intellectuals (Africans and non-Africans) engaged in the study of Africa. This section stresses the imperative of reflexivity by examining the roles of African and Africanist intellectuals in decolonization, as well as putting the question of decolonizing knowledge in deep philosophic terms. This ordering allows us to pose questions that cut across modes of inquiry (the arts, media, philosophy), rather than isolating them.

By offering a collection of essays that foregrounds this struggle across many disciplines, we outline some of the ways in which intellectual practice can serve to de-link Africa from its global representation as a debased, subordinated, deviant, and thus inferior entity. It is in this sense that George Hartley strongly links post–World War II American imperialism with this ongoing colonial history in his discussion of Malcolm X's attempts to conscientize African Americans to the links between their oppression and the colonization of the African continent. Similar to Malcolm X's warning against the attempts of the popular media to "psycho" African Americans into unconsciousness about post–World War II imperialism in Africa, T. Spreelin MacDonald shows in his chapter the intellectual legacy of the South African Black Consciousness leader Steve Biko, and how Biko's legacy has been passed down within literary discourse as the imperative to continually assert intellectual independence from psychic domination by prevailing public discourses.

Lest we assume that Africa has escaped this human-inhuman dichotomy that European colonization ushered in during the intervening decades, as Steve Odero Ouma and Adebisi Olawuyi argue in their respective chapters, the popular media are saturated with images of Africa as a failed, debauched, and consummately unmodern place. In Ouma's terms, the West is prevalently cast as "Dr. West," attending to a chronically, perhaps terminally ill Africa, thus reinforcing the conception of Africa as inherently inferior and dependent upon the West. Ouma argues that through this and similar stereotypes, media representations serve to elide critical engagement with African realities, stating: "Generalizations and stereotypes, once deeply entrenched in the minds of persons, invariably create conditions that engender explanatory constructs . . . rather than inquisitorial constructs seeking to investigate the reasons behind events or certain behaviors."

Janet Hess further argues in her chapter that this trope of African illness and deficiency filters into common representations of African liberation movements and their leaders, such as Ghana's Kwame Nkrumah and the Congo's Patrice Lumumba, as "failures." As Hess shows, this "failure" is largely the product of a hierarchy in which African liberation leaders are judged against a Western masculine norm predicated upon the essential ability to "triumph." In contexts in which the utopian goals articulated during the struggle for independence were compromised, this norm has served to cast such leaders and their nations as failures.

Hess's chapter suggests that colonial tropes of African sickness and failure are instrumental in the continual subjugation of African liberation to the conceptual apparatus of colonialism. Similarly, Western gender norms imported through colonialism continue to abort such independence. Chapters by Oyèrónké̩é̩ Oyěwùmí and Marlene De La Cruz-Guzmán, respectively, forcefully make this point. Through a critique of Western scholarship on Africa, and especially Yoruba visual arts, Oyěwùmí's chapter demonstrates the manners in which Western gender constructs have been naturalized within scholarship of African arts, locking their interpretation into a Western gaze that functions to produce its own obscuring myths about African aesthetics and artistic practices, and eliding the crucial observation that "gender dichotomies are not inherent in any art form; rather, gender models are part of the critical apparatus that they have inherited from the European and American intellectual tradition, and they must be recognized as such."

De La Cruz-Guzmán's chapter dis-covers, in Enrique Dussel's term, the disconnect between nationalist rhetoric about women in Zimbabwe before, during, and after the independence struggle, and it highlights the betrayal of women in the context of liberation rhetoric and discourse. She uses Yvonne Vera's novels *Nehanda* and *The Stone Virgins* to dis-cover the postcolonial mythology and lack of decolonization for the average Zimbabwean woman, while also providing a link for potential cooperation and solidarity with other women across the continent and the world. Like De La Cruz-Guzmán's discussion of the fractures between decolonization and elite nationalist rhetoric, Lesley Cowling and Carolyn Hamilton further draw out the contradictions and struggles within contemporary South African public discourse, in which public intellectuals and the postapartheid government have waged running battles over the meaning and practice of South Africa's political decolonization.

In sum, all of the chapters presented here speak to the friction between intellectual practice and received (colonial) notions of Africa, be they mainstream images of debauchery and destruction presented by popular media, or still-existent colonially derived constructions of gender, race, and postcoloniality underpinning much of the academic discourse on Africa. Thus, in modeling emancipatory readings of African cultural and philosophical practices, these chapters map out a range of ways forward in so decolonizing Africa. As Serequeberhan asserts: "Just as the political and armed struggle ended the de facto actuality of colonialism, the critical-negative project of African philosophy has to challenge and undo the de jure philosophic underpinnings that justified this now defunct actuality and still today sanction Western hegemony. And this, by extension, is applicable *grosso modo*, to all intellectual work on Africa." Thus decolonization must be further understood as the struggle to realize African humanity on its own terms, realizable, fundamentally, in the realm of intellectual practice.

A luta continua!

Notes

1. Frantz Fanon, *Black Skin, White Masks*, trans. Charles Lam Markmann (Paris: Éditions du Seuil, 1952; New York: Grove Press, 1967), 232. Citations refer to the Grove Press edition.

2. Ngũgĩ wa Thiong'o, *Decolonizing the Mind: The Politics of Language in African Literature* (Nairobi: East African Educational Publishers, 1986), 4.

3. Fanon, *Black Skin, White Masks*, 232.

4. Frank B. Wilderson III, "Biko and the Problematic of Presence," in *Biko Lives!: Contesting the Legacies of Steve Biko*, ed. Andile Mngxitama, Amanda Alexander, and Nigel C. Gibson (New York: Palgrave, 2008), 111.

5. Emmanuel Eze, *Achieving Our Humanity: The Idea of the Postracial Future* (New York: Routledge, 2001), 168.

6. Oyèrónké̩é̩ Oyěwùmí, *The Invention of Women: Making an African Sense of Western Gender Discourses* (Minneapolis: University of Minnesota Press, 1998), 23–24.

7. Mogobe B. Ramose, *African Philosophy Through Ubuntu* (Harare: Mond Books, 1999); V. Y. Mudimbe, *The Invention of Africa: Gnosis, Philosophy, and the Order of Knowledge* (Bloomington: Indiana University Press, 1988).

8. Aimé Césaire, *Discourse on Colonialism* (New York: Monthly Review Press, 2004), 54–55.

9. Amílcar Cabral, *Return to the Source: Selected Speeches* (New York: Africa Information Service, 1973); Cabral, *Revolution in Guinea: Selected Texts* (New York: Monthly Review Press, 1972); Cabral, *Unity and Struggle: Speeches and Writings* (New York: Monthly Review Press, 1979).

10. See Andrew Roberts, ed., *The Colonial Moment in Africa: Essays on the Movement of Minds and Materials, 1900–1940* (Cambridge: Cambridge University Press, 1990).

Part I

Representation and Retrospection

We Need a Mau Mau in Mississippi

Malcolm X's Political Lessons for Today

George Hartley

On December 20, 1964, at the Audubon Ballroom in Harlem, Malcolm X declared, "Oginga Odinga [the vice president of recently liberated Kenya] is not passive. He's not meek. He's not humble. He's not nonviolent. But he's free."

This fact was part of a larger object lesson that Malcolm X had for black Americans:

> [Jomo Kenyatta, Oginga Odinga, and the Mau Mau will] go down as the greatest African patriots and freedom fighters that that continent ever knew, and they will be given credit for bringing about the independence of many of the existing independent states on that continent right now. There was a time when their image was negative, but today they're looked upon with respect and their chief is the president and their next chief is the vice president.
>
> I have to take time to mention that because, in my opinion, not only in Mississippi and Alabama, but right here in New York City, you and I can best learn how to get real freedom by studying how Kenyatta brought it to his people in Kenya, and how Odinga helped him, and the excellent job that was done by the Mau Mau freedom fighters. In fact, that's what we need in Mississippi. In Mississippi we need a Mau Mau. In Alabama we need a Mau Mau. In Georgia we need a Mau Mau. Right here in Harlem, in New York City, we need a Mau Mau.
>
> I say it with no anger; I say it with very careful forethought.[1]

The most important insight of Malcolm X's speeches and writings during the last two months of his life concerns the relationship between the African diaspora's struggles against internal colonialism in the United States and the liberation movements' struggles against European colonialism and U.S. neocolonialism on the African continent. The key here is the recognition that blacks on both continents are fighting the same enemy—the white power structure of capitalist imperialism. While the civil rights movement in the United States emphasized an integrationist ethos that implicitly shored up the interests of the U.S. elite, Malcolm X fought not for a *civil* rights movement but for a *human* rights movement, having learned from the examples of Patrice Lumumba and Jomo Kenyatta that a truly independent African socialism depends on the forceful resistance to colonialism.

As noted above, not long before his assassination, Malcolm X told black America that in Mississippi, in Alabama, in Georgia, and in Harlem, "we need a Mau Mau." His message to black America was that black liberation was possible in the United States as well as in Kenya, Ghana, and the Congo; that the African American struggle was part of the global struggles against imperialism; that "the revolution on the outside of the house" was troubling enough for the power structure, but they were then "beginning to see that this struggle on the *outside* by the black man is affecting, *infecting* the black man who is on the *inside* of that structure" (*MX*, 160–61, emphasis added). The influence of the African liberation movements has, in his words, never been fully told, and black *America* needs to follow black *Africa's* example and answer the racist violence of the white man with "vigorous action in self-defense" (164–65).

The greatest lesson for us to draw today from the speeches and interviews of Malcolm X from December 1964 to his death in February 1965 is to recognize the analytical and synthesizing moves of the argument he developed during this crucial period. This is especially true for his analysis of U.S. intervention in the Congo. These moves will allow us to draw similar conclusions regarding the intimate ties between imperialism abroad and imperialism here at home.

The most important element of the colonization of the mind—which is the main point underlying Malcolm X's analysis—is the role of the press in shaping public opinion, in particular the public opinion of Afro-Americans. It is through the press that the U.S. government and the imperialist power structure are able to "psycho"

black consciousness, to brainwash Afro-Americans into internal-
izing the colonial mythologies that justify the status quo, including
the systematic violence that polices and maintains that status quo.
Just as important, however, Malcolm X also developed a process
of *decolonizing* black minds, and that involved seeing through the
smokescreen created by the press and identifying with the struggles, methods, and achievements of the African liberation fighters
such as the Mau Mau in Kenya and the Simbas in the Congo. As he
put it:

> When you begin to start thinking for yourself, you frighten
> them, and they try and block your getting to the public, for
> fear that if the public listens to you, then the public won't
> listen to them anymore. . . . And if you don't develop the
> analytical ability to read between the lines in what they're
> saying, I'm telling you again—they'll be building gas ovens,
> and before you wake up you'll be in one of them, just like the
> Jews ended up in gas ovens over there in Germany. You're in
> a society that's just as capable of building gas ovens for Black
> people as Hitler's society was.[2]

Relationship between the African Revolution and the Afro-American Struggle

What "we know too little about," Malcolm X told his audiences, "is
our relationship with the freedom struggle of people all over the
world" (*MX*, 117). In particular, he emphasized

> the importance of realizing the direct connection between
> the struggle of the Afro-American in this country and the
> struggle of our people all over the world. As long as we think
> . . . that we should get Mississippi straightened out before we
> worry about the Congo, you'll never get Mississippi straight-
> ened out. Not until you start realizing your connection with
> the Congo. . . .
> When I speak of some action for the Congo, that action
> also includes Congo, Mississippi. But the point and thing that
> I would like to impress upon every Afro-American leader is
> that there is no kind of action in this country ever going to

bear fruit unless that action is tied in with the over-all international struggle. . . .

I might point out here that colonialism or imperialism, as the slave system of the West is called, is not something that is just confined to England or France or the United States. The interests in this country are in cahoots with the interests in France and the interests in Britain. It's one huge complex or combine, and it creates what's known not as the American power structure or the French power structure, but an international power structure. This international power structure is used to suppress the masses of dark-skinned people all over the world and exploit them of their natural resources, so that the era in which you and I have been living during the past ten years most specifically has witnessed the upsurge on the part of the black man in Africa against the power structure. (*MX*, 90, 89, 160)

Analysis of the Trickery in the Congo: Manipulation by the Press

Malcolm X spoke of the "step-by-step" process used by the press:

First they [fan] the flame in such a manner to create hysteria in the mind of the public. And then they shift gears and fan the flame in a manner designed to get the sympathy of the public. And once they go from hysteria to sympathy, their next step is to get the public to support them in whatever act they're getting ready to go down with. You're dealing with a cold calculating international machine, that's so criminal in its objectives and motives that it has the seeds of its own destruction, right within. (AB)

Those seeds of destruction included the Afro-Americans' dawning recognition of their relationship to African liberation movements. But a major task of Malcolm X's analysis was to explain the apparent lack of sympathy by black America concerning the slaughter of black Africans. The major mystery, which he took on in his analysis of the situation regarding the Congo, was the fact that despite the mass murder taking place in an African country as Western planes dropped bombs on Congolese villages, killing black men, women, and babies, there was no "outcry, no sympathy, no support, no concern" expressed by Afro-Americans. What could account for this lack of international racial solidarity? Malcolm X's answer was the "trickery" of the press in the service of imperialism. Afro-Americans do not sympathize because, in his words, "the press didn't *project* it in such a way that it would be designed to get your sympathy. They know how to put something so that you'll *sympathize* with it, and they know how to put it so you'll be *against* it" (AB, emphasis added).

The recognition of this ability and willingness by the press to manipulate public emotion and opinion was the first point in Malcolm X's decolonizing analysis of the relationship between Africa and Afro-America. This manipulation involved, among many things, the choice of loaded descriptors: the bombing was a "humanitarian project"; the planes were flown by "American-trained anti-Castro Cuban pilots"; they were doing it "in the name of freedom." Malcolm X asked, "You see how step-by-step they grab your mind" with this propaganda? These glorious terms "are used to pave the way in your mind for what they're going to do" (AB).

The next point, the counterpoint, in Malcolm X's decolonizing analysis was to offer an alternative description of these events and actors that better explained the power dynamics at play:

> These pilots are hired, their salaries are paid by the United States government. They're called mercenaries, these pilots are. And a mercenary is not someone who kills you because he's patriotic. He kills you for blood money, he's a hired killer. This is what a mercenary means. And they're able to take these hired killers, put them in American planes, with American bombs, and drop them on African villages, blowing to bits Black men, Black women, Black children, Black babies, and you Black people sitting over here cool like it doesn't even involve you. You're a fool. They'll do it to them today, and do it to you tomorrow. Because you and I and they are all the same. (AB)

Next, Malcolm X explained what has since come to be known as a classic "postcolonial" situation: In order to legitimate its colonialist interventions, the U.S. government handpicks a criminal to prop up as leader of the newly independent state, someone who allows U.S. interests unfettered access to the resources of the nation, cracks down on his own people when they protest, and allows foreign military forces to operate within the country. In the case of the Congo, Malcolm X explained:

> They take Tshombe.... He's the worst African that was ever born.... He's the murderer of Lumumba ... the first and only rightful prime minister of the Congo.... The United States takes him, puts him over the Congo, and supports his government with your tax dollars.... His salary's paid by the United States government.... His first move is to bring in South Africans, who hate everything in sight. He hires those South Africans to come and kill his own Congolese people. And the United States, again, pays their salary. (AB)

Malcolm X explained that this justification of the installation of Tshombe as the only African who could "bring unity to" the Congo was really just a cover for their real reason for imperialist interest in the country, which was to recapture the country in order to exploit its vast mineral resources, to take advantage of its strategic geographic location as a base for intervention in other African countries, and to counter the inspiration of the Congolese liberation fighters who would support other African nations in their wars against colonialism.

Another cynical move by the press was their lack of coverage of the thousands of dead Congolese blacks while decrying the capture of white hostages: "A white skin is more valuable than a . . . black skin. This is what they're implying! . . . They're vicious in their whiteness" (AB). The most insidious effect of this press manipulation, however, was that the other side of *projection* is *internalization*. Given the three- to four-century history of seeing negative images of Africa and Africans projected in the Western press, the Afro-American has tended to internalize these negative images. Malcolm X described this process:

> They always project Africa in a negative light: jungle savages, cannibals, nothing civilized. Why then naturally it was so negative that it was negative to you and me, and you and I began to hate it. We didn't want anybody telling us anything about Africa, much less calling us Africans. In hating Africa and in hating the Africans, we ended up hating ourselves, without even realizing it. Because you can't hate the roots of a tree, and not hate the tree. You can't hate your origin and

George Hartley / 21

not end up hating yourself. You can't hate Africa and not hate yourself. . . .

And this is what the white man knows. So they very skill-fully make you and me hate our African identity, our African characteristics. . . . It made us feel inferior; it made us feel inadequate; made us feel helpless. And when we fell victims to this feeling of inadequacy or inferiority or helplessness, we turned to somebody else to show us the way. (*MX*, 168, 169)

Manipulation by the Government

Like the mainstream Western media, the government of the United States was a tool for imperialist control of the globe. And like the media, the government played its own role in the "trickery" involv-ing perceptions, sympathies, antipathies, and ultimately action—or more often inaction. As Malcolm X explained, "After 1959 the spirit of African nationalism was fanned to a high flame and we then began to witness the complete collapse of colonialism" (*MX*, 169–70). Be-cause the European countries that were losing territory and influ-ence across the globe were so thoroughly identified with imperialism, international capital had to find a new governmental vehicle to carry on its legacy, a government that was not so obviously identified with the history of Western imperialism.

As Malcolm X put it, "They pulled a trick that was colossal. . . . They passed the ball to Uncle Sam. And he picked it up and has been running it for a touchdown ever since" (*MX*, 170). And in this case it was the Africans who, according to Malcolm X, had internalized the propaganda of the West: "At that time, the Africans couldn't see that though the United States hadn't colonized the African continent, it had colonized 22 million blacks here on this continent. Because we're just as thoroughly colonized as anybody else" (170).

This crucial move in Malcolm X's argument worked in two direc-tions at once, alerting the newly independent African nations to their colonial kinship to blacks in America, while at the same time alerting blacks in America to their own colonial condition and therefore to their kinship to the decolonizing movements in Africa.

President Kennedy played a pivotal role in Malcolm X's argument, for Kennedy was the figure who, having caught the ball, scored against Africans and Afro-Americans at the same time. And this analytical move of X's provided a hinge point for comparing the trickery concerning perceptions of Africans and Afro-Americans. Kennedy's great propagandistic ploy in Africa was the creation of the Peace Corps, and with it the move from an openly militaristic form of imperialism to an apparently benign form. In X's words, "They came up with some benevolent colonialism, philanthropic colonialism, humanitarianism, or dollarism. Immediately everything was Peace Corps, Operation Crossroads, 'We've got to help our African brothers.' Pick up on that. Can't help us in Mississippi. Can't help us in Alabama, or Detroit, or out here in Dearborn where some real Ku Klux Klan lives" (*MX*, 170–71). So in this way the United States could pose as humanitarians and still end up controlling the resources of Africa. According to X, "This country can seduce God. Yes, it has that seductive power—the power of dollarism. You can cuss out colonialism, imperialism and all other kinds of isms, but it's hard for you to cuss that dollarism. When they drop those dollars on you, your soul goes" (199). And so, through the seemingly benevolent ideology of progress and development, the United States could gain strategic influence over many a postcolonial African leader.

Analysis of the Trickery at Home

In the same way Kennedy, according to Malcolm X, was able to seduce the leaders of the civil rights movement here at home. JFK "specialized in how to psycho the American Negro" (*MX*, 173). Malcolm continued:

> Kennedy's new approach was pretending to go along with us in our struggle for civil rights. He was another proponent of rights. But I remember the expose that *Look* magazine did on the Meredith situation in Mississippi. *Look* magazine did an expose showing that Robert Kennedy and Governor Barnett had made a deal, wherein the Attorney General was going to come down and try to force Meredith into school, and Barnett was going to stand at the door, you know, and say, "No, you can't come in." He was going to get in anyway, but it was all arranged in advance and then Barnett was supposed to keep the support of the white racists, because that's who he was upholding, and Kennedy would keep the support of

the Negroes, because that's who he'd be upholding. It was a cut-and-dried deal. And it's not a secret; it was written, they write about it. But if that's a deal, how many other deals do you think go down? (*MX*, 173)

The U.S. media are equally effective in their collusion with such government trickery in their depiction of conditions here at home as they are abroad, especially in the maintenance of the government's monopoly on violence. Whether it is South Vietnam, South Africa, or South Carolina, the situation is the same—the brutal suppression of people of color by whites in positions of power. "But when it comes time for you and me to protect ourselves against lynchings," Malcolm X pointed out, "they tell us to be nonviolent." He continued:

That's a shame. Because we get tricked into being nonviolent, and when somebody stands up and talks like I just did, they say, "Why, he's advocating violence." . . . I have never advocated any violence. I have only said that black people who are the victims of organized violence perpetrated upon us by the Klan, the Citizens Councils, and many other forms, should defend ourselves. And when I say we should defend ourselves against the violence of others, they use their press skillfully to make the world think that I am calling for violence, period. I wouldn't call on anybody to be violent without a cause. But I think the black man in this country, above and beyond people all over the world, will be more justified when he stands up and starts to protect himself, no matter how many necks he has to break and heads he has to crack. (*MX*, 164)

The manipulative lever for this move is to the diversionary tactic of characterizing black self-defense as racist and "violence in reverse." And as before, this projection of a negative image becomes internalized by black Americans:

This is how they psycho you. They make you think that if you try to stop the Klan from lynching you, you're practicing "violence in reverse." Pick up on this, I hear a lot of you all parrot what the man says. You say, "I don't want to be a Ku Klux Klan in reverse." Well, you—heh!—if a criminal comes around your house with his gun, brother, just because he's got a gun and he's robbing your house, brother, and he's a robber, it doesn't make you a robber because you grab your gun and run him out. No, see, the man is using some tricky logic on you. And he has absolutely got a Ku Klux Klan outfit that goes through the country frightening black people. Now, I say it is time for black people to put together the type of action, the unity, that is necessary to pull the sheet off of them so they won't be frightening black people any longer. That's all. And when we say this, the press calls us "racist in reverse."

"Don't struggle—only within the ground rules that the people you're struggling against have laid down." Why, this is insane. But it shows you how they can do it. With skillful manipulating of the press, they're able to make the victim look like the criminal, and the criminal look like the victim. (AB)

The press distortion of the riots during the summer of 1964 provided Malcolm X with a powerful example of this projection/internalization tendency:

I was in Africa, I read about [the riots] over there. If you noticed, they referred to the rioters as vandals, hoodlums, thieves, and they skillfully took the burden off the society for its failure to correct these negative conditions in the black community. They took the burden completely off the society and put it right on the community by using the press to make it appear that the looting and all of this was proof that the whole act was nothing but vandals and robbers and thieves, who weren't really interested in anything other than that which was negative. (*MX*, 166)

And according to Malcolm X, some black Americans accepted this characterization of the riots and repeated it themselves. Malcolm X countered this version with the socioeconomic context of the riots: far from participating in random, senseless violence, the rioters, because they could not get to the white landlords and store owners who profited daily from the institutionalized racial violence against blacks in America, instead targeted their property, the sites of racialized economic exploitation.

The inescapably exploitative nature of capitalism is the final connection between Africa and Afro-America that this chapter will address. Capitalism, Malcolm X told us, is a vulturistic system, a system of bloodsuckers (*MX*, 121). For this reason, he suggested:

All of the countries that are emerging today from under the shackles of colonialism are turning toward socialism. I don't think it's an accident. Most of the countries that were colonial powers were capitalist countries, and the last bulwark of capitalism today is America. It's impossible for a white person to believe in capitalism and not believe in racism. You can't have capitalism without racism. And if you find one and you happen to get that person into a conversation and they have a philosophy that makes you sure they don't have this racism in their outlook, usually they're socialists or their political philosophy is socialism. . . .

We pray that our African brothers have not freed themselves of European colonialism only to be overcome and held in check now by American *dollarism.* Don't let American racism be "legalized" by American dollarism. (*MX*, 69, 75)

Lessons from Malcolm X

My overall point is that this kind of analysis that Malcolm X put to work in his speeches during the final two months of his life provides us with crucial lessons for today. The Western press and the United States government still function at the behest of the capitalist system, the international imperialist power structure of U.S. corporations. Capitalism is still racialized in order to function as a divide-and-conquer strategy of the rich against the poor. The power plays at home still have intimate connections to the same power plays abroad.

The demonization by the press and our government of the new socialist leaders in Latin America works hand in hand with anti-Arab and anti-Mexican racism in the United States. The rape of the environment in the Middle East by oil companies is intimately connected to global climate change, resulting in the increased frequency and magnitude of hurricanes in the Gulf of Mexico, revealing the relationship between indigenous Alaskans whose lives are disrupted by melting ice caps and poor people in New Orleans whose lives were ended by Hurricane Katrina. Then add the manipulation by the press in its portrayal of blacks "looting" stores in a crime spree while whites were simply "finding" food in these same stores in their attempt to survive.

Malcolm X's analytical strategy is helpful in showing the connections between the U.S. government's so-called "War on Drugs" in the

Andes; the rise of right-wing death squads in that region; the demonization of the democratically elected Socialist presidents of Venezuela,
Ecuador, and Bolivia; and the crack boom in poor urban neighbor-
hoods in the United States. How coincidental is the connection between the boom in heroin production in Afghanistan since the U.S.
invasion and the boom in heroin consumption in poorer communities
in the United States itself, such as in Athens County, Ohio, where I
am writing from?

And finally, what does it mean, from Malcolm X's perspective,
that the president of the United States is the child of a Kenyan father
and a Euro-American mother—some of whose family members were
slave owners while others fought against the South during the Civil
War? What would Malcolm X make of this person who, on the one
hand, symbolizes the rise from slavery to the presidency, but who, on
the other hand, occupies the role of commander in chief of imperialism? An African American who expresses heartfelt concern for the
downtrodden while promising to bomb the people of Afghanistan?
An African American who will oversee the exploitation of Nigerian
and Venezuelan oil? We might finally have an African American in the
White House, but will we have a Mau Mau in Mississippi?

Notes

1. Malcolm X, *Malcolm X Speaks: Selected Speeches and Statements,* ed.
George Breitman (New York: Merit, 1965), 106 (hereafter cited as *MX*).
2. Malcolm X, "After the Bombing / Speech at Ford Auditorium," tran-
scribed and edited by the Malcolm X Museum and Noaman Ali, http://
www.malcolm-x.org/speeches/spc_021465.htm (hereafter cited as AB).

Nkrumah/Lumumba

Representations of Masculinity

Janet B. Hess

In 1958, Ghanaian prime minister Kwame Nkrumah maintained before the African People's Conference that "the independence of Ghana will be meaningless unless it is linked up with the total liberation of Africa. . . . There have been great Empires on this African continent, and when we are all free again, our African personality will once again add its full quota to the sum of man's knowledge culture."[1] Patrice Lumumba similarly argued in 1958 that "the present dream of Africa, of all of Africa, including the Congo, is to become a free and independent continent, like all the other continents of the world, for it is the will of the Creator that all men and all peoples be free and equal."[2] Despite their intellectual and political vision, Lumumba and other leaders of the decolonization era are often cast as tragic figures. As one historian stated, Julius Nyerere's Tanzania constitutes "a case study of misplaced idealism, lost developmental opportunities, and unfulfilled political promises. . . . There is little disagreement about the moral content of Nyerere's thought and his vision of a just and prosperous society. The same cannot be said for the means selected and results obtained in pursuit of this dream."[3]

In this chapter I would like to discuss representations of intellectual leaders of the independence era—specifically, visual representations of Kwame Nkrumah and Patrice Lumumba—and the reception and translation of those representations into an ideology of tragedy constructed around Western notions of masculinity. Michael Leja has argued that ideology can constitute "an explicit, consciously held set of beliefs and commitments organized around a political affiliation," but it can also be seen as "an implicit structure of belief, assumption, and disposition—an array of basic propositions and attitudes about reality, self, and society embedded in popular representation and discourse and seemingly obviously true and natural."[4] Constructions of masculinity are historical,[5] and the ways we see and apprehend information are also historical. Apprehending and interpreting the intellectual legacies of Nkrumah, Lumumba, Nyerere, and other figures of the decolonization era involve acknowledging the layers of Western interpretation and representation surrounding these figures, including constructs of media, masculinity, and modernization.

Attention to the individual human body has been discussed by many theorists as critical in addressing the maintenance and dissemination of power. Victor Turner has described the human body as "the symbolic stage upon which the drama of socialization is enacted."[6] Bill Nichols elaborates, "Economies of colonization or . . . corporeal management, operate to take over effective control of the body, to safeguard it, to regulate its activity, to oversee its movements. . . . The body is the battle site of contending values and their representation."[7] If the practices and discourses related to the body are considered in the social and historical context of decolonization, it is clear that the representation and comportment of the body were significant in the establishment of a particular vision of the colonized and "nationalized" subject. The body surface is a uniquely important focus for the configuration of identity and gender: fantasy and bodily ideals are reshaped, and local visions and histories of desire are advanced, in the site of the colonized and decolonized body. Such visions and histories have a profound impact upon both historical narrative and personal identity. As Irit Rogoff suggests, "We actively interact with images from all arenas to remake the world in the shape of our fantasies and desires [and] narrate the stories which we carry within us."[8]

Colonial and Neocolonial
Constructions of the Body: Nkrumah

The dissemination of specific ideals and values related to masculinity, and the socialization through discourse related to the body of "nationalized" subjectivity and identity, is exemplified in the visual culture of the African independence era. Prior to independence, and for much of the colonial period, Western authorities enforced the belief that mere physical proximity to the bodies of inhabitants of the west coast of Africa was enough to induce illness in expatriate populations. In Accra, Kumasi, and Dar es Salaam, for example, separate living sectors were established for the British and local populations. Only after the 1923 publication of the Devonshire White Paper was this policy abandoned, as the White Paper maintained:

> It is now the view of the competent medical authorities that, as a sanitation measure, segregation of Europeans and Asiatics is not absolutely essential for the preservation of the health of the community.... It may well prove that in practice the different races will, by a natural affinity, keep together in separate quarters, but to effect such segregation by legislative enactment except on the strongest sanitary grounds would not, in the opinion of His Majesty's Government, be justifiable.[9]

Representations of the educated and modern urban subject in the visual culture of the independence era initially projected resistance to colonial "economies of colonization" by means of assimilation and conformity to European standards. Advertisements from the time period immediately preceding Ghanaian independence reveal a physical ideal closely allied with the objectives of industry and capitalism. In an advertisement for the Bank of West Africa, for example, both worker and manager present an "up-to-the-minute" impression in crisp Western suits and ties, an image illustrating the message that "the rapidly expanding economy of Ghana in which we operate, offers excellent opportunities to enterprising firms."[10] Early representations of Nkrumah, showing the Convention People's Party candidate in a Western-style suit and tie, reinforced these attributes of Westernization and modernity, while advertisements for retail services—such as that in the *Daily Graphic* for the Kingsway Department—drew together ideological discourses related to Western dress, commerce, and modernity.[11]

As the works of Karen Hansen and Michela Wrong demonstrate, correlations between the adornment of the body and constructions of identity and gender are local, temporal, and subject-specific.[12] In the newly independent nations of Africa, masculinity, modernity, and nationalism have come together in complex significations of authority and African identity. A clear example of this convergence of ideological influences is the comportment and dress of government officials in the independence era. In the official presidential portrait disseminated by the Nkrumah administration, for example, President Nkrumah's shoulder and lower body are draped in kente; yet his shirt is neither a Western collared business shirt nor a shirt from northern Ghana, as the curious polka-dot pattern reveals, but a collarless garment of the type associated with a Socialist leadership.[13] Nkrumah would appear to be projecting several messages simultaneously, bearing the emblem of a range of Ghanaian and non-Ghanaian cultural practices, traditional attire, and clothing associated with non-African political regimes.

The publication New Ghana similarly contains carefully orchestrated cultural representations conforming to specific audiences and occasions. In a photograph published in New Ghana, Nkrumah appears during a trip to Balmoral Castle in the U.K. attired in a Western suit and carrying a cane. The caption reads "Prince Philip and Dr. Kwame Nkrumah share a joke about the Prime Minister's walking stick";[14] the primary source of amusement today is the fact that it is Prince Philip in a Scottish kilt who appears to be attired in "tribal" attire. A photograph of Nkrumah at the old British colonial polo grounds in Accra—dated March 5, 1957—shows Nkrumah and his compatriots declaring the independence of Ghana, and attired in the men's tunic of the Northern Territories.[15] The same attire is captured in a photograph of Nkrumah, the minister of justice, Kofi Ofori Atta, and other officials celebrating the thirteenth anniversary of "positive action";[16] the event is staged for the crowd at the Accra Sports Stadium, but as well for the Ghanaian cameramen documenting the event, and the photographers of New Ghana.[17]

The adornment of women's bodies also suggests the coming together of nationalist sentiments, political objectives, and transnational modernity. At parades, conventions, and demonstrations, Ghanaian women appeared in textiles manufactured abroad and printed with the portrait of Nkrumah.[18] The massing together of women at events celebrating independence and the redundant representation of his image—like the twentieth and twenty-first-century replication in textiles of photographs of the Asantehene Prempeh I, Otumfuo Opoku Ware II, and Osei Tutu II—suggest the kind of sensorial overload once associated exclusively with the Asante Odwira.

The Nkrumah administration also had an effect on the performative depictions and capacities of the body. An illustration by the independence-era artist known as Ghanatta depicts Nkrumah with his head configured in the shape of the nation of Ghana; he is Ghana, in the manner in which he is represented.[19] In the CPP Manifesto of 1954, Nkrumah's body defines the boundaries of the continent of Africa;[20] an editorial illustration of 1964 depicts his facial features in the shape of the continent. Nkrumah's body posture also projected his relative authority and identity.[21] Numerous photographs and editorial illustrations issued in government publications show Nkrumah striding forward as his subjects kneel or bow in reverence,[22] while Nkrumah is depicted as enormous in size. The emphasis on Nkrumah's body as the central site for commentary is also suggested by illustrations produced after the coup of 1966; Nkrumah is portrayed in a range of publications as obese, monstrous, or otherwise grotesque.[23]

Liberation and Cinematic Representations of Masculinity: Lumumba

In the postcolonial West, representations of African masculinity have achieved a resonance markedly different from constructed images in the immediate aftermath of liberation. In marked contrast to the notion of nationalism symbolized by the physical comportment of African intellectuals in the era of liberation—signifying both modernity and the coalescence of regional authority—Western representations of independence-era leaders have functioned to emasculate or diminish their authority. In Western cinematic representations of Africa, this diminishment is evidence of a long-standing colonizing impulse. Laura Mulvey argues in her classic analysis of visual colonization, "Visual Pleasure and Narrative Cinema," that "the fascination of film is reinforced by preexisting patterns of fascination already at work within the individual subject and the social formations that have molded him."[24] Although Mulvey analyzes colonizing desire in terms of male domination, her analysis may be usefully applied to the fascination with, and related effort to dominate, the African body. As Mulvey states, the dominant social actor "controls the film fantasy and also emerges as the representative of power in a further sense: as the bearer of the look of the spectator, transferring it behind the screen to neutralize the extradiegetic tendencies represented by woman [read: African] as spectacle."[25]

In Mulvey's formulation, the dominant position of the film spectator replicates the voyeuristic gaze of a patriarchal social order. As Mulvey argues, "Cinematic codes create a gaze, a world, and an object, thereby producing an illusion cut to the measure of desire."[26] Fantasies of domination are projected upon the female form in film, but the woman serves as a constant threat of potential loss of authority: "She also connotes something that the look continually circles around but disavows: her lack of a penis, implying a threat of castration and hence unpleasure. . . . Thus the woman as icon, displayed for the gaze and enjoyment of men, the active controllers of the look, always threatens to evoke the anxiety it originally signified."[27] A similar replication of the scopic regime of Western culture may be observed in presentations and representations of the body; as cinema's "formal preoccupations reflect the psychical obsessions of the society which produced it,"[28] the vision of Africa and African masculinity depicted in Western cinema is one of excess and the drive for surveillance and containment.

Mulvey's analysis of the voyeuristic and colonizing effects of cinematic representations of Africa provides a valuable perspective from which to view the revisionism of Raoul Peck's documentary *Lumumba: La Mort du Prophete*, which subverts dominant representations of the Congolese leader Patrice Lumumba.[29] In his documentary, Peck employs the medium of documentary to insert himself within a biographical and poetic account of Lumumba's assassination. Western cinematic presentations of Africa offer, with respect to such shattering and pivotal international incidents, a deafening silence. As Manthia Diawara explains,

> For political reasons, the former colonizers do not want to see the retelling of African independence stories on film. Insofar as such a story is told from the perspective of the postcolonial filmmaker and depicts the former colonizers and oppressors and violators of human rights, it is unacceptable to the West, which would rather deny that past. . . . Any artistic representation of independence contributes a challenge to . . . [the] totalizing image of the West . . . as champions of human rights and democratic views.[30]

Peck's haunting and lyrical account of Lumumba's role in the independence of the Congo is a startling instance of this transgressive representation. The filmmaker's grief at Lumumba's death is personal and palpable as he recounts the devastating consequences of Lumumba's loss: "In Katanga, it is said that a giant fell in the night. And the water that falls from the heavens, from the forehead, the water that falls from the eyes . . . All these waters cry plaintively where death has the face of a giant. In Katanga, if one tells you, mother, pointing with the finger, this is the spot where the child lies, don't believe a word, mother, not a word. . . . It was a giant, my mother, a giant who fell that night, that night in Katanga."[31]

Documentary is a self-consciously personal genre well-suited to the discourse of decolonization, as Diawara has argued: "The voice of the filmmaker signals his presence in the film, placing him in relation to the subject of the film. . . . The filmmaker questions other people's memories of independence, archival material, and monuments of history."[32] In shots of anonymous passersby in the rainy cityscapes of Belgium, in interviews with bureaucrats, politicians, and journalists, and in footage from his childhood in the Congo, Peck dramatically contrasts received cinematic narratives of Africa with historical and archival memory. Diawara argues that "the incommensurability between the political history of the continent and its artistic history" has been the consequence of suppression by Western economic and media interests.[33] Peck's film represents a triumph in its depiction of independence, which "finally provide[s], for a brief moment, the most important occasion for Africans to reclaim artistic agency."[34]

In the last moments of *Lumumba: La Mort du Prophete*, the camera pans over the site of the Belgian Place des Martyrs, its name a wrenching and ironic allusion to the footage of a bound Lumumba being led to his execution. The film suggests, however, the possibility of resurrection for the Congo as Peck narrates, "A prophet foretells the future. But the future has died with the prophet. . . . Today, his sons and daughters weep, without ever having known him. His message has vanished, but his name remains. Should the prophet be brought back to life again?"[35] Lumumba himself anticipated the Western narrative of a defeated and broken Congo, and both Peck's film and Lumumba's final message refuse this subversion of agency. In the final letter he wrote shortly before his death, Lumumba shares:

> My beloved companion,
>
> I write you these words not knowing whether you will receive them, when you will receive them, and whether I will still be alive when you read them. . . . Whether dead or alive, free or in prison by orders of the colonialists, it is not my person that is important. What is important is the Congo. . . . I know and feel in my heart of hearts that sooner or later my

people will rid themselves of all their enemies, foreign and domestic, that they will rise up as one to say no to the shame and degradation of colonialism and regain their dignity in the pure light of day. . . . I want my children, whom I leave behind and perhaps will never see again, to be told that the future of the Congo is beautiful and that their country expects them, as it expects every Congolese, to fulfill the sacred task of rebuilding our independence, our sovereignty; for without justice there is no dignity and without independence there are no free men.

Neither brutal assaults, nor cruel mistreatment, nor torture have ever led me to beg for mercy, for I prefer to die with my head held high, unshakeable faith and the greatest confidence in the destiny of my country rather than live in slavery and contempt for sacred principles. . . . Do not weep for me, my companion, I know that my country, now suffering so much, will be able to defend its independence and its freedom. Long live the Congo! Long live Africa![36]

The West—and, through dissemination of Western representations of Africa, much of the world—has inherited and received the notion that the leaders of the independence era failed. The Western model of masculinity necessarily requires a demonstration—indeed, almost a physical and bodily rehearsal and enactment—of triumph. The rhetoric of leaders of the independence era is perceived as inspiring, but their project is construed as a failure. The dream of Lumumba died, and we avert our eyes. But surely this narrative is a function of the misrepresentation and misconstruction of masculinity, and the neutralizing, as Mulvey argues, of the extradiegetic power of the African intellectual and the African body in cinematic representation. What is the true message of Nkrumah and Lumumba's legacy? That they and their colleagues failed, and that a heightened level of Western intervention is needed?

The message instead, we can understand today, is a transformative vision, a vision of individual traditions coming together, being circulated and reconstructed, reborn. Manthia Diawara posits:

One can say that, having died, Nkrumah, Lumumba and Toure are no longer individuals; they have become myths; they symbolize Africa as a whole; they are the dream of African unity. But our shining truth in Africa lies in the independence movements they led; this is where our search for liberty and equality in the world must begin. . . . To deny us the history of our independence is to insist that we have no subjectivity, and to state that we are unworthy of freedom and equality. The West should reconcile itself with this truth without feeling that in so doing, it is threatening its own sense of justice and democracy.[37]

Notes

1. Kwame Nkrumah, quoted in Okwui Enwezor, *The Short Century: Independence and Liberation Movements in Africa, 1945–1994* (New York: Prestel, 2001), 365–66.

2. Patrice Lumumba, quoted in *Lumumba Speaks: Speeches and Writings of Patrice Lumumba, 1958–1961*, ed. Jean Van Lierde (Boston: Little, Brown, 1972).

3. Rodger Yeager, *Tanzania: An African Experiment* (Boulder, CO: Westview Press, 1982), 1.

4. Michael Leja, *Reframing Abstract Expressionism: Subjectivity and Painting in the 1940s* (New Haven, CT: Yale University Press, 1993), 6.

5. Robert W. Connell, "The History of Masculinity," in *The Masculinity Studies Reader*, ed. Rachel Adams and David Savran (Malden, MA: Blackwell, 2002), 245–61.

6. Victor Turner, quoted in *Clothing and Difference: Embodied Identities in Colonial and Post-Colonial Africa*, ed. Hildi Hendrickson (Durham, NC: Duke University Press, 1996), 2.

7. Bill Nichols, *Representing Reality: Issues and Concepts in Documentary* (Bloomington: Indiana University Press, 1991), 238.

8. Irit Rogoff, "Studying Visual Culture," in *The Visual Culture Reader*, ed. Nicholas Mirzoeff (London: Routledge, 1998), 26.

9. Richard Brand, "A Geographical Interpretation of the European Influence on Accra, Ghana, Since 1877" (PhD diss., Columbia University, 1972), 44.

10. Directory of the Republic of Ghana, 1961/62, 91.

11. *Daily Graphic* (Accra, Ghana), February 6, 1957, 5.

12. Karen T. Hansen, "Second-Hand Clothing Encounters in Zambia: Global Discourses, Western Commodities, and Local Histories," *Africa: Journal of the International African Institute* 69, no. 3 (1999): 343–65; Michela Wrong, "A Question of Style," *Transition* 80 (2000): 18–31.

13. Emmanuel D. Ziorklui, *Ghana: Nkrumah to Rawlings* (Accra: Em-Zed Books, 1993), 34.

14. *New Ghana*, 1959, 1.

15. Enwezor, *The Short Century*, 191.

16. *New Ghana*, January 8, 1963.

17. Ibid., January 30, 1963.

18. *Evening News* (Accra, Ghana), March 7, 1962, 6.

19. Janet B. Hess, *Art and Architecture in Postcolonial Africa* (Jefferson, NC: McFarland, 2006), 65–69, 106–13.

20. *Guinea Times*, March 3, 1985, 5.

21. *Evening News*, May 10, 1954, 2.

22. Ibid., February 10, 1964, 3.

23. Ibid., June 1, 1963, 10.

24. Laura Mulvey, "Visual Pleasure and Narrative Cinema," in *Narrative, Apparatus, Ideology: A Film Theory Reader*, ed. Philip Rosen (New York: Columbia University Press, 1986), 198. Chapter originally published as article in *Screen* 16, no. 3 (1975): 6–18.

25. Ibid., 204.

26. Ibid., 208.

27. Ibid., 205.

28. Ibid., 200.

29. Raoul Peck, dir., *Lumumba: La Mort du Prophete* (San Francisco: California Newsreel, 1992).

30. Manthia Diawara, "African Cinema and Decolonization," in Enwezor, *The Short Century*, 347–48.

31. Peck, *Lumumba*.

32. Diawara, "African Cinema," 349.

33. Ibid., 346.

34. Ibid.

35. Peck, *Lumumba*.

36. Patrice Lumumba, quoted in Enwezor, *The Short Century*, 184–85.

37. Diawara, "African Cinema," 350.

Trauma and Narrativity in Adichie's
Half of a Yellow Sun

Privileging Indigenous Knowledge in
Writing the Biafran War

Marlene De La Cruz-Guzmán

Chimamanda Ngozi Adichie's *Half of a Yellow Sun* highlights the relevance of trauma theory and the decline of postcolonial Nigerian nationalism that opens narrative space for formerly marginalized voices
from the Biafran War.[1] As Senan Murray noted, quoting fellow Nigerian writer Dulue Mbachu, "After a war is fought, the victors immediately write their history. But it takes a while for the victims to find
their voice and tell their own side story."[2] Thus, trauma theory and
the concept of witness or *testimonio* literature will be used to explore
the paradigm of "double traumatization" of the character Ugwu and
its consequences for Nigerian civil society, and these will authenticate
and provide clinical support for Adichie's representation of trauma
in her second novel. In addition, this article will explore the novel's
three-part move toward indigenous knowledges by highlighting first
the writing of the modernist grand narrative, then its flawed internal
critique in terms of the postmodernist counternarrative, and, finally,
by beginning to explore and open the possibility for privileging indigenous knowledges that are better suited to the Nigerian post–
Biafran War conditions.

The theoretical paradigm of double traumatization in relation to
postcolonial texts allows this article to open a new space for the
analysis of previously marginalized voices, which are now being ac-
knowledged and validated in the process of clarifying that their experiences stem from two separate but intertwined assaults on their

existence and that detraumatization can begin with writing. I assert that the indigenous Nigerian populations, to whom Adichie gives voice in her literary works, have experienced a double traumatization, which, including a postindependence decline in nationalism and outright civil war in Biafra's attempt to secede, fosters an environment in which peoples who were first assaulted by European colonial forces suffer a second, even more difficult, betrayal trauma from the most unexpected source: fellow indigenous people working under the banner of Nigerian nationalism.

While the first betrayal strengthened the various indigenous people's reliance on one another both as members of the oppressed community and as potential partners in the fight for independence, the second betrayal seemed to alienate and obliterate their basic belief in and practice of community and solidarity among and within the groups. This psychic shift, an additional detrimental side effect of the assaults, is particularly relevant in an analysis of the character of Ugwu, arguably the least logical choice in the novel of an author who strives to provide a voice for marginalized women. But it is this very illogicality that renders this study able to draw a more thorough analysis of the double traumatization experienced by all the testimonio-providing characters in *Half of a Yellow Sun*.

To analyze the components of double traumatization and the interconnectedness of these two traumas, I must first survey the field of trauma theory and then make clear the departures and new contributions of the double traumatization theoretical framework. Post-traumatic stress disorder (PTSD) was officially included under its current name in the *Diagnostic and Statistical Manual of Mental Disorders* (*DSM-III*) published in 1980. This inclusion, along with its fourteen years of subsequent revisions and updates to create *DSM-IV*, published in 1994, has legitimated the diagnosis of this mental health disorder and has, even more important for this project, expanded its diagnosis beyond war-ravaged individuals. In fact, the *Journal of Traumatic Stress* and *PTSD Research Quarterly* were both created to provide a new space in which to consider broader PTSD research.

In its post–*DSM-IV* form, PTSD's definition has been expanded so that the qualifying trauma is no longer only war-related but can emerge from any "trauma inducing experiences such as rape, abuse, disasters, accidents, and torture."[3] This expanded definition, which still requires a traumatic trigger for the series of symptoms, has given way to a new critical trend in literature, namely trauma theory, which is often identified with Dominick LaCapra's and Cathy Caruth's work. While Caruth still relies heavily on a Freudian cosmology for her treatment of trauma in narratives and narrative trauma, she has opened an important space for scholars to build on trauma theory and create new theoretical paradigms for postcolonial studies.

Lenore Terr's definition of trauma is most appropriate for the literary texts at hand: "'Psychic trauma' occurs when a sudden, unexpected, overwhelming intense emotional blow or a series of blows assaults the person from outside."[4] Judith Herman further posits that it is an assault that causes fear and terror.[5] Thus, for the purpose of this study, literatures of trauma are those that deal with overwhelming assaults from outside or their aftermath of fear and terror. Often these literatures focus on war and its effects on the human psyche.

Standing on the shoulders of Western giants such as Freud and Pierre Janet, however, is a dangerous proposition for the postcolonial scholar, who must step away to change the symbolic representations to reflect appropriate indigenous or Creole cosmologies and key figures for symbolic representation of the "abnormal traumas (war, genocide, political violence, untimely death)," which Caruth grounds in Freudian terms.[6] Thus, the key figures in this analysis and Adichie's novel are particularly Nigerian culture-specific and not oedipal.

The assertion that postcolonial peoples are recovering from a double traumatization in this paper is a unique contribution to the field of trauma studies, which has been mostly associated with the study of the Holocaust and the Vietnam War, and has thus limited its application to other global events such as the original German holocaust perpetrated against the Herero people of Namibia and the massacres of indigenous peoples in Matabeleland, Zimbabwe. This new critical framing of trauma allows a unique approach to inform the novel of Adichie as testimonio literature and to deconstruct the multiple traumas inflicted upon the main characters that provide their counternarratives to previously accepted history as well as a turn toward indigenous knowledges at the end of the novel.

In this conception of double traumatization in a postcolonial and postnationalist environment, the culturally specific concept of indigenous knowledges in Igbo society is privileged in the framing and renegotiation of the Freudian concept of traumatic repetition, so that it is applicable and pertinent to this culturally specific analysis of a West African narrative. This article attempts to intentionally reject the hegemonic application of Western critical thinking in favor of more culturally driven theoretical frameworks that engage the literary texts in more relevant and critically useful ways that privilege the indigenous authors, cultures, and histories and open spaces for formerly marginalized voices in the postcolonial world.

In a postcolonial setting, there is always an original trauma that causes PTSD: colonial rule. Thus, colonization imprints a first traumatic assault on the minds of the previously subjugated indigenous peoples. As a coping mechanism, however, individuals cling to their communities and their sense of interdependence with other human beings to reaffirm their own humanity and to stand against the hegemonic powers that choose to devalue their humanity. This first betrayal strengthens the people's reliance on one another both as members of the oppressed community and as potential partners in the fight for survival and independence. However, the PTSD is evident in their daily lives as intrusive memories and flashbacks, emotional numbing, avoidance, and an exaggerated startled response to stimuli betray the individual's mental health disorder.

In the case of the British colony of Nigeria, its own communally sound forms of government were eradicated in favor of a cheaper hegemonic government instituted by the colonizers. For instance, according to the British, "in the Southeast, the Igbo lived in small republican communities. They were nondocile and worryingly ambitious. Since they did not have the good sense to have kings, the British created 'warrant Chiefs,' because indirect rule cost the Crown less" (*HY*, 147) and, not surprisingly, allowed for minimal involvement in politics but major export of valuable resources and capital. Based on this concept of indirect rule, "in 1914, the governor-general joined the North and the South, and his wife picked a name. Nigeria was born" (147), as one state encompassing a myriad of ethnic communities.

The various indigenous groups had coexisted before, but the burdens of exploitative colonialism stressed their relationships; and the "divide-and-rule" (*HY*, 209) policies of the colonial government kept the groups from uniting to fight for independence, equality, and peace. However, even when they were able to live and strive for independence together, the animosity between the groups, who were now forced to work together, was still an undercurrent in their dealings with one another. As a useful illustration, they would work together and socialize, but intermarriage among the groups was strongly discouraged. Thus, these harmful resentments and animosities were nurtured by the colonial rule and produced a series of PTSD symptoms in relation not only to the British, the brutal oppressors, but also to fellow indigenous groups that were seen to be more or less collaborative in the colonial system and to benefit in direct relation to their collaboration. Thus, postindependence Nigeria would carry with it the burdens of the colonial divide-and-rule policies.

Furthermore, I have added a claim of double traumatization in *Half of a Yellow Sun* defined here as two distinct yet incremental sets of experiences that cause fear and terror and are outside the normal range of human experience, which when combined produce a damaged psyche. The second trauma is categorized as betrayal trauma, which is unique because "the people or institutions we depend on for survival violate us" and "the core issue is betrayal—a betrayal of trust that produces conflict between external reality and a necessary system of social dependence."[7] In this narrative context, avoidance, amnesia, and pathological dissociative responses that help the individual keep threatening information from awareness are triggered by the betrayal. Furthermore, there is a loss of volume control and traumatic reenactment that compels the victim to repeat the action without knowing that he or she is repeating it because it is his or her way of remembering. Thus, the double traumatization model developed here implicitly includes colonialism as the first trauma factor and betrayal trauma as the second factor, and in doing so, complicates the normal treatment of literature through the critical lens of trauma theory. Furthermore, I argue that writing serves as detraumatization for Adichie and the Igbo people.

In this context of double traumatization, Chimamanda Adichie's novel serves as catharsis for the many ethnic groups categorized as "Nigerian," who suffered the first trauma of a colonial invasion and its subsequent oppression and a second betrayal trauma delivered by the Nigerian army's suppression of the Biafran secession attempt. As an indigenous woman, a descendant of the secessionists, Adichie is a direct descendant of the originally traumatized and granddaughter of those who participated in the Biafran secession.[8] Thus, it could be argued that she is part of the collectively traumatized indigenous people of Nigeria and is thus uniquely poised to write this narrative. In other words, she provides the words and thoughts that Ugwu strives to write at the end of the novel.

By rejecting Caruth's claim that literature should be reread as an extension of Freudian studies of trauma,[9] and privileging Fanon's concept of a black man's "neurotic" condition,[10] a psychoanalytic approach to the study of Adichie's novel and its various characters, but with a non-Western set of key figures for symbolic representation of the war, genocide, political violence, and untimely death, is hereby employed. Thus, the key figures in this text are particularly Nigerian and Igbo culture-specific, not oedipal. Therefore, the roaches, chickens, herbs, swarms of flies, and harmattan winds are used by Adichie because they resonate within the Nigerian and African symbolic discourse. Consequently, the different expressions of post-traumatic stress syndrome are acculturated to this West African setting as well.

In this narrative context, avoidance, amnesia, and pathological dissociative responses that help the individual to keep threatening information from awareness are triggered by creating "a disruption in the usually integrated functions of consciousness, memory, identity, or perception of the environment."[11] In the case of Ugwu's character, who has experienced a myriad of Nigerian and Biafran lifestyles, including those of privileged civilian, deprived civilian, unwilling soldier, corrupt soldier, rapist, lover, servant, and village boy, there is a loss of volume control, also known as a distorted internal system of arousal, that allows his psyche to register harmless people or events as viable threats, and a repetition compulsion that becomes the victim's way of remembering. The combination of the latter changes Ugwu and his fellow Biafran soldiers from victims to victimizers as they become addicted to trauma as a soothing and stimulating mechanism,[12] so they remove themselves from the role of victims in the secession struggle they are losing and assume the power of those who terrorize and abuse others—the very reason why the Igbo strove to secede.

Thus, this double traumatization and inability to heal themselves lead them to the most disturbing outcome: a state of being both "a fragile spider" that fears being easily erased and a "hungry, predatory spider" that inflicts further trauma on others. The spider metaphor is used here to resonate with Yvonne Vera's use in her novels as well as the work of Tsenay Serequeberhan, for the spider image foregrounds the idea that these characters' psyches provide the source of their own change from victims to victimizers. They, "like the proverbial spider, always [spin] the thread of its web out of itself. It forgets this at its own peril, at the risk of being snared by its own mesh."[13] However, in Adichie's use of a spider image, the spider is ultimately in control and confidently at home in its web, as we see reflected in Ugwu's healing psyche at the end of the novel (*HY*, 522).

This disjuncture is at the crux of Adichie's narrative, for it truly opens spaces for the most marginalized of voices, and it authenticates the counternarratives of all the survivors, including the most problematic figures, such as Ugwu, while ultimately moving toward a privileging of indigenous knowledges. The perspective of these narratives insists on acknowledging colonial hegemony and violence, yet also reiterates the double culpability of these brutally oppressive European systems and their legacy in modeling and creating a new indigenous people who moved from victim to victimizer under the auspices of nationalist and/or separatist ideologies that betrayed and marginalized the very people they were supposed to unite. Thus, postcolonial literatures and indigenous narratives are in a unique position to decentralize Western epistemology and produce a countermemory that contradicts the perpetrators' grand narrative. It also opens critical spaces for the retelling of a more inclusive, independent, indigenous narrative. That space is used to explore the range of actions of Ugwu's character because Adichie positions him as a victim turned victimizer who finds a way beyond the modernist and postmodernist narratives to seek the indigenous knowledges that he must find and privilege at the end of the novel. Therefore, Ugwu, like his fellow victims and victimizers, is uniquely poised to provide insights into the mind of a Nigerian/Biafran character who has experienced betrayal trauma.

The first trauma to the indigenous people of Nigeria was the imperialist racism, categorization of ethnic groups, and superimposed unity in 1914 as a Nigerian colony. The British consolidation of these groups into a colony resulted in what psychiatrist Hussein Abdilahi Bulhan categorized as "the generalization, institutionalization, and assignment of values to real or imaginary differences between people in order to justify a state of privilege, aggression, and/or violence. Involving more than the cognitive or affective content of prejudice, racism is expressed behaviorally, institutionally, and culturally."[14] Thus, in Nigeria, various indigenous peoples were grouped together under British rule and assigned subhuman value, following which their only purpose was to be to abandon their own culturally rich traditional ways and strive, instead, to be good Christian, English-speaking laborers and servants to the colonists and missionaries. In the process of establishing a colony of indirect rule, the British illegitimately assigned Igbo chiefs as low-cost administrators for the everyday control of the colony so that, as Achebe points out, there was no king in Ogidi, but colonialism put the king back for its own profit and destroyed indigenous common law.[15]

Frantz Fanon appropriately argued that since the indigenous person "lives in a society that makes his inferiority complex possible, in a society that derives its stability from the perpetuation of this complex, in a society that proclaims the superiority of one race; to the identical degree to which that society creates difficulties for him, he will find himself thrust into a neurotic situation."[16] This original assault on the indigenous person's dignity and humanity leaves him or her traumatized and with limited possibilities of recovery if rebellion is suppressed and submission demanded. However, a sense of community among the people as oppressed subjects of the British Crown and as potential partners in the fight for freedom serves as a coping mechanism. The various groups of people unite in a liberation struggle because the "neurotic situation was simply unbearable, and the people, especially in rural areas, still had clear connections to their ancestors and traditional ways. As Bulhan posits, even today, "the world is still reeling from the historical avarice and violence Europe unleashed upon it.... Europe's greed to own and control has had a profound impact on human history and psyches."[17] However, the assignment of chiefs under indirect rule also forced this elite group within the greater population to suffer a colonization of the mind and an identification with all that is British to a greater extent than to that which is indigenous. Thus, for the rest of the population, excluding this elite group, colonialism produced PTSD as freedom fighters struggled for a postcolonial nation free of colonial hegemony.

Adichie's novel successfully lays the groundwork for an understanding of this legacy of European extraction of resources and continued exploitation of the African continent with Nigeria as a case study, for it clearly shows the grand narrative of colonial domination and its legacy. Chief and Mrs. Ozobia are introduced in the second chapter of the novel as the collaborator-beneficiaries of the colonial system who still benefit in a postindependence scenario from their acceptance of the title of chief and British hegemonic practices.

Two descriptions of the couple by British observers provide an insight into their standing in society and their relation to the former colonizers. Susan Grenville-Pitts, from the British Council, describes them in relation to Kainene when she says,

> Her mother is stunning, absolutely stunning. Chief Ozobia
> owns half of Lagos but there is something terribly nouveau
> riche about him. He doesn't have much of a formal education,
> you see, and neither has his wife. I suppose that's what makes
> him so *obvious*. *(HY, 74)*

Thus, Susan is completely unimpressed with their pedigree because they are too "*nouveau riche*" and lack a Western education, although she admires their actual wealth and exercise of power. However, her description reveals a very British perspective that chooses
to gloss over facts, such as that Ozobia is newly rich because the
British placed him in this position of privilege during the colonial
period; and he lacks education because this was not an option open
to him since he was actually busy doing the day-to-day administering of the colony for the British mission of indirect rule instead of
grounding himself in his own indigenous knowledges or immersing
himself in formal British education. In other words, this is a luxury
that was not available to him if he was to grab at the power that the
British offered him. Furthermore, the mind-set behind her assessment is still that of a British colonialist, for she says of the different
indigenous groups, "The Hausa in the North were a dignified lot,
the Igbo were surly and money-loving, and the Yoruba were rather
jolly even if they were first-rate lickspittles" *(HY, 69)*. Thus, her assessment of Ozobia is in keeping with her stereotypes of the larger
Igbo group.

Richard Churchill, a new arrival to Nigeria who is drawn to the
country by the ninth-century art of the roped pot instead of its people,
is a failure in England and decides to travel to Nigeria to write about
the ancient art of the area. A failure in the homeland, he looks to the
African continent as an escape. This is the description of Chief Ozobia
that the narrator provides through Richard's eyes, and, I would argue,
one very akin of a museum description of an artistic piece depicting
these individuals:

> Chief Ozobia looked expansive, with the arching hand ges-
> tures he made as he spoke, the intricately embroidered *agbada*
> whose folds and folds of blue cloth made him even wider than
> he was. Mrs. Ozobia was half his size and wore a wrapper and
> headgear made out of the same blue fabric. . . . How perfectly
> almond-shaped her eyes were, wide-set in a dark face that
> was intimidating to look at. *(HY, 74)*

He focuses solely on the physical dimensions of these characters, in stark contrast to his lover's description of their status in society, and he provides an artistic rendering of their deportment. Still, the fact that two Brits are bothering to provide portraits of the couple indicates their importance in both local and international society as vehicles through which extraction of valuable resources can be mediated for the benefit of the neocolonial powers.

Thus, when Olanna is noted to be Chief Ozobia's daughter in the airport, she is immediately offered: "Well done, madam. I will ask the porter to take you to the VIP lounge" (*HY*, 33), because all chiefs and their families were to be treated with deference and to be courted for their powerful connections with the British and their more direct rule of their area. Her mother and father continue to keep the invented title of chief and take advantage of it for business purposes. In addition, just as they had been willing to trade their allegiance to their own Igbo people and to pretend that they were rightful and traditional holders of the chief titles the British offered them in exchange for administering an exploitative system of colonialism, they were now willing to trade their daughters for business contracts. Olanna wondered "how her parents had promised Chief Okonji an affair with her in exchange for the contract. Had they stated it verbally, plainly, or had it been implied?" (39). She does not question their practices or attempt to make them aware of their continued colonial legacy of privilege. Instead, she simply and quietly refuses to submit to their demands. In addition, she does not try to disavow them of their notions of "a proper university in Britain" as the best option for Nigerians but still takes a post at Nsukka, the first indigenous university in the country, despite her father's comment that it was a "silly" idea (40).

Chief Ozobia and his wife engage in corrupt business negotiations so that Chief Okonji, a fellow betrayer of the indigenous Igbo, makes Olanna an offer: "I can arrange for them to buy from your father at five or six times the price" (*HY*, 41), in exchange for her sexual attention. Furthermore, like her parents, he is willing to put his own desires above the good of the nation, which is now under majority rule and poised to succeed with its own administration of economics and resources, including oil. This is what she calls, "the gloss that was her parents' life" (42). Thus, he offers, "I can appoint you to a board, any board you want, and I will furnish a flat for you wherever you want" (41), without particular concern for his role as a civil servant or his country's need for solid administration but rather as an immediate means for his sexual gratification. Thus, the corruption that Adichie makes apparent through the chief characters in the novel also allows the reader to see the grand colonial narrative that gave these individuals titles and power of exploitation, and undermined indigenous communal practices in order to gain profit. In addition, it also points to their promotion in the new nationalist postindependence paradigm to cabinet ministers and the like so that the postcolonial future of the people of Nigeria under their rule is nearly as grim after independence as it was before, for it is fully a legacy of colonialism.

The second assault on the postcolonial indigenous people of Nigeria was the betrayal trauma inflicted by the very nationalist forces that were supposed to unite under indigenous majority rule all Nigerian people regardless of ethnic affiliation, bring a more equitable distribution of resources to the dispossessed, and restore dignity to the majority of people and their indigenous customs. Thus, Adichie's novel depicts "post-independent Nigeria, at a time when colonialism's heirs—corruption, political strife, and religious dogmatism—strain family and community."[18]

As noted, chiefs such as Ozobia and Okonji demonstrate a focus on self-aggrandizement and selfishness so that their concerns, as key ruling elite in the new postcolonial nation, are not for the nation's growth and development into a decolonized state that honors indigenous knowledges but rather a continuation of the exploitative practices of the colonial system that benefited them so. Thus, when Olanna complains about the pictures taken of her at parties, which her mother carefully orchestrates, she says that the photographer, like the average Nigerian, "would never understand the discomfort that came with being a part of the gloss that was her parents' life" (*HY*, 42), because this was the life everyone aspired to, with pictures in the magazines, glamorous social engagements, and enough money to travel the world, gain an education, and be truly independent. It is important to note here that Ozobia and his wife have not used these profits to help their fellow Nigerians or even their extended family members, such as Uncle Mbaezi, but have kept it close to the nuclear family, in a very Western model of individual pursuit and enjoyment of wealth.

Olanna often makes major decisions that go against her parents' wishes, including rejecting marriages with other chiefs' sons and joining the Students' Movement for Independence at Ibadan, but "still, . . . the disapproval made her want to apologize, to make up for it in some way" (*HY*, 43). Thus, she is clearly experiencing a colonization of the mind, as described by Ngũgĩ, and evidenced by her perfect British accent, Western education, and her self-aggrandizing notions of herself as "not white" and as a nationalist. Thus, she provides a counternarrative to her parents' grand narrative, but as an insider critique, she does not call for a dismantling of the colonial infrastructure and legacy that keep her parents in social and economic power in postcolonial Nigeria. Instead, she passively disobeys their requests and voices bland criticisms and flimsy requests for her parents to acknowledge their own privilege and to be less entitled. However, her useless requests, such as the one to thank the servants because "Olanna wished they would; it was such a simple thing to do, to acknowledge the humanity of the people who served them" (37), are not only disregarded but also serve as opportunities for her parents to reinscribe their privilege and their entitlement in the postcolonial Nigeria, just as they had during the colonial era in which they also profited.

Kainene's questioning of her parents' entitlement is more aggressive yet equally useless since it, too, is an internal postmodern critique. Thus, she asks, "So will you be spreading your legs for that elephant in exchange for Daddy's contract?" (*HY*, 44), and later tells Richard, "My sister and I are meat. We are here so that suitable bachelors will make the kill" (73). However, she still shows up to the parties when her parents ask and allows photographers to take pictures. Ironically, she assumes the responsibilities of her father's business in the south and will, presumably, conduct business in a similar manner as "Kainene is not just like a son, she is like two" (39). In another expression of useless revulsion against their parenting, "Kainene used to say their mother's breasts did not dry up at all, that their mother had given them to a nursing aunt only to save her own breasts from drooping" (48), but she does not then move to honoring Aunt Ifeka as a second mother and questioning her mother's choices. Instead, she simply ignores both women as much as possible and seeks to follow in her father's business steps.

Given this home environment, Olanna's only connection to her indigenous Igbo roots comes from her uncle Mbaezi, who lives in Kano in the north and has not bought into the Western ideas of government or business because he is too rooted in the daily life of the community in which he lives. In other words, he is worried about the daily worries of the Igbo living in the northern Hausa and Muslim part of the country. The concerns, for instance, are centered on the daily life difficulties such as Igbo students not being allowed into schools in the north, so he, as leader of the Igbo Union, fund-raises and organizes to build the Igbo Union Grammar School on Airport Taxi Road. He is a man of substance with a strong working family anchored in communal Igbo life and not a man of society or business in the Lagos style. Thus, Olanna's visits to see him and his family anchor her in a more realistic environment of Igbo life that is, ironically, not lived on Igbo land.

Her aunt and uncle reflect the community that made it possible to preserve their community, ancestral, and indigenous connections to one another even under colonialism, and their communal living, in the compound in Sabon Gari, and even now in their everyday words such as "I am even better now that I see you" (*HY*, 48), and "May another person do for you" (49). In addition, they forgo their own comfort for the love of others and share their communal home so that "Uncle Mbaezi and Aunty Ifeka slept on mats, next to the many relatives who always seemed to be staying with them" so that she, the visiting relative, could sleep in their bed (49). It is only here that she feels a sense of grounding so that "she felt a sense that things were in order, the way they were meant to be, and that even if they tumbled down once in a while, in the end they would come back together again. This was why she came to Kano: this lucid peace" (49).

It is in Kano that she also experiences a happy intermixing of ethnic groups, so that "she wished she were fluent in Hausa and Yoruba, like her uncle and aunt and cousin were, something she would gladly exchange her French and Latin for" (*HY*, 50). Here, her family intermingles with non-Igbo while never neglecting their own indigenous roots so that she is able to see how postindependence Nigeria could work well if the government were able to shun corruption and to focus on the good of the people of all ethnic groups who must, given the modern demands of the nation, live together and share community life. In Kano, Abdulmalik is the representative of the Hausa-speaking neighbors just as Ibiba is the representative Ijaw living in the compound. Abdulmalik has a stall in the market along with her uncle, and he engages in commerce with everyone and spends much social time with her Igbo relatives.

However, the undertones of interethnic conflict are just under the surface even here in Kano, as evidenced by the need for the Igbo school and Arize's comment that "Papa would kill me first of all if he knew I was even looking at a Hausa man" (*HY*, 52). Furthermore, part of the ritual Kano trip is a visit to Mohammed's home so that Olanna says of his mother, "I am no longer the Igbo woman you wanted to marry who would taint the lineage with infidel blood," and he responds, "Your parents felt the same way as she did" (57). Thus, even this haven for Olanna houses the same problematic interethnic tensions of the rest of the nation.

In spite of herself, however, Olanna brings her parents' lifestyle baggage with her when she visits Kano. Thus, she notes Abdulmalik's stained teeth, is bothered by the smoke in the kitchen and by the cockroach eggs under the table so that "the smoke irritated her eyes and throat [and] the sight of the cockroach eggs nauseated her. She wanted to seem used to it all, to this life" (*HY*, 52); however, she is not used to it, because she is the daughter of a chief, who now profits from business life in Lagos and has been removed from the ordinary, daily Igbo life that she experiences in Kano. This is a life that she both yearns for, as an alternative to her parents' glossy socialite lives, and is repulsed by in the actual lived reality and lack of comforts. Thus, even when she visits Kano, she remains a pampered guest who demands visits to tourist sites, is cooked for, allowed to sleep on the bed, and given presents by family friends. She is not an integrated member of the community, so she has no community responsibilities that tie her to the people she visits. In fact, she simply benefits from what she calls a "lucid peace" (49) as a reprieve from Lagos, and the reader can't help but connect this privilege with her own parents' status among the Igbo.

Thus, when she says to Mohammed that she is not like white people, the grand narrative that the chief has tried to pass on to her, he responds with a postmodern assertion: "Of course you're not. You're a nationalist and a patriot, and soon you will marry your lecturer the freedom fighter" (*HY*, 58). Yet, she is still, like Mohammed, the beneficiary of the colonial legacy of indirect rule; and, also like him, she is shaped by the system so that she, again like him, can offer only a weak internal critique of the system without ever really threatening to dismantle or even make visible the infrastructure of hegemony once instituted by the British colonizers but now kept alive by their parents, who benefit immensely from the corrupt system and pass on those benefits to them as their offspring.

The critique of postmodernism is also evident in Olanna's and Kainene's passive critiques of their parents' grand narrative of hegemony that privileges only them because they do not actually strive to change the status quo. Thus, Adichie's choice to first show the modernist narrative via the parents, the daughters' own mild and superficial criticisms, without accompanying action and without dedication to change so that they might rightfully be called nationalists or patriots, renders them useless weak critics of the grand narrative and of Nigerian politics and governance—or, simply put, postmodernists instead of postcolonialists.

Meanwhile, in Nsukka, the reader faces the indigenous intellectuals who also offer postmodernist critiques of the system but fail to stay connected to their indigenous roots. Thus, while Odenigbo is keen on Ugwu's getting an education, he focuses on the British schooling that he considers so important. He initially warns that "there are two answers to the things they will teach you about our land: the real answer and the answer you give in school to pass" (*HY*, 13–14); but he fails to keep Ugwu focused on the real answer because he is no longer connected to his own indigenous roots. In fact, he never tries to integrate Ugwu's indigenous knowledges into the equation of education, and this reveals his comments to be simplistic postmodernist critiques of the system without any activism or postcolonial engagement to change the system to include indigenous experiences. Additionally, he is ultimately advising Ugwu to comply with the hegemony of the educational system in order to get ahead, just as he has. Thus, despite his own views of himself as a patriot and a nationalist, he is deeply engrossed in postmodernism and not in a move toward privileging indigenous knowledges.

Odenigbo's comment that the Germans "started their race studies with the Herero and concluded with the Jews" (*HY*, 63), a striking parallel to Césaire's argument in *The Discourse on Colonialism*,[19] is an insightful comment that reveals an ability to move beyond Western paradigms of thinking, unlike Miss Adebayo, who cannot fathom the connection, and to provide meaningful critiques of European hegemony that reveal the infrastructure of domination patterns and the abuse of the African continent. Thus, theoretically, he moves beyond superficiality in the assessment of greater continental patterns. However, he fails to do so in his analysis of the Nigerian nation, his own homeland. Odenigbo is then caught in the web of postmodernism, which does not allow for the real emancipation of his homeland.

Odenigbo as well has too much distance from that which is truly local or indigenous, for, as he says about the local fruit but could also say about lived indigenous practices, "No, no, . . . local pineapples are

too acidic, they burn my mouth" (*HY*, 113). Thus, he is able to acknowledge that there are indigenous ways, but he still rejects them in
favor of the Western ways he has learned in his assimilated educated
circle. Ironically, Odenigbo is still a "revolutionary" because he questions the status quo even if only superficially, and that is more than
most do. Thus, he advocates for an indigenous university in Nsukka,
but he helps to mold the students into Western intellectuals who, like
him, will offer only weak critiques of the colonial legacy of the system
after colonialism. In other words, his critique of the system and its
colonial origins is too weak because it comes from the inside and he,
like his fellow intellectuals, benefits from its continuation.

Adichie's skillful novel then turns to the experience of the Biafran
War, in which the key figures are exposed to their indigenous Igbo
roots in such a way that they must opt for a move away from postmodernism and the privileging of indigenous knowledges as the way
to go forward. Of particular interest in this journey is Ugwu, who
illustrates the entire cycle because he came from the village at the
beginning of the novel, learns Western ways under Odenigbo's and
Olanna's tutelage while serving as their "houseboy," serves in the Biafran army, and then returns to a more indigenous and thus grounded
and complex understanding of the problems that plague his nation.
Therefore, by the end of the novel he is the one preparing to write a
book about Nigeria.

Ugwu begins his journey as "one of these village houseboys" (*HY*,
16) who is eager to please the master, to mimic the master's demeanor
and language, and to succumb to the master's Western ways to the
same degree that he rejects those of his own family and village. Thus,
he agrees to go to school, to read books, to learn to cook Olanna's
Westernized dishes, and to follow Western norms of hygiene, including women's "scented powder for his armpits and . . . two capfuls of
Dettol in his bath" (60). Ugwu is subject to the modernist presump-
tion that his ways are backward and must thus be changed to accom-
modate the new, more Western, university environment that he now
inhabits. However, living with Odenigbo also entails learning that
such norms must be questioned and/or critiqued.

Life with Odenigbo and Olanna proves an interesting proposition
for Ugwu, who is caught in the middle of their Western assumptions
of how daily life should be conducted, which forms the infrastructure
of their household. Thus, there is a need for a "village houseboy" as
a well-treated servant, and a directive that education should be the

priority even if money is unavailable because, as Odenigbo indicates in his rant against Ugwu's impecunious parent, "'your father should have borrowed!' . . . and then, in English, 'Education is a priority! How can we resist exploitation if we don't have the tools to understand exploitation?'" (*HY*, 13).

Of course, after his university education, Odenigbo seems to have forgotten life in Abba and the effects on a family of a year's failed crops. He also seems to forget that while he is paternalistic toward Ugwu and offers him education, he is still using his fellow countryman, his "good man," as a servant in the tradition of the British who colonized Nigeria and exploited their labor. Olanna, as indicated above, has no reference point other than this modernist grand narrative that her parents provided for her. Thus, she quickly engages in her own attempts to make Ugwu more Western and more acceptable to her tastes as a modern, educated, wig-wearing Nigerian woman. In other words, the couple have fallen victims to the pitfalls of national consciousness, as outlined by Frantz Fanon in *The Wretched of the Earth*, because "the native bourgeoisie which comes to power uses its class aggressiveness to corner the positions formerly kept for foreigners,"[20] instead of using its power to align with the needs of the masses.

An internal critique of modernism is certainly posed by both Odenigbo and Olanna, especially the former, who is avant-garde in his critical political observations of all of Africa. However, they both question while still benefiting from the system. They do not attempt to break down the infrastructure of the colonial legacy in the postcolonial period. For instance, while in Kano, Olanna is upset that the beggars outside Mohammed's compound do not move to beg from a woman like herself. Thus, "Olanna wanted to put some money in their bowls but decided not to. If she were a man, they would have called out to her and extended their begging bowls" (*HY*, 54). She feels justified in not giving them alms because of their sexist behavior. However, she does not question why the societal infrastructure allows for beggars when her ex-lover, just inside those same gates at which these men beg, drives a foreign sports car and possesses unlimited family wealth and power. Just as she does with her own family, Olanna seems capable of placing only minor self-centered critiques of the system that do not threaten the unjust infrastructure of the postcolonial nation she inhabits or the power of her family and her friends.

For an application to Ugwu's lived experience, the example of Ugwu's natural body odor as a working man is a useful one. Olanna, newly returned from getting a university education in England, is offended by Ugwu's natural body odor. Thus, she cajoles him into taking measures to prevent it. When Odenigbo questions her about the new "flowery scent on my good man," she asks whether he had noticed the strong odor, and he answers, "That's the smell of villagers. I used to smell like that until I left Abba to go to secondary school. But you wouldn't know about things like that" (*HY*, 61). Thus, she, who thinks she does her bit for justice by thanking her employees for their services, is ignorant about the everyday lives of the majority of the population. She is appalled at natural body odor, which, as Odenigbo points out, is perfectly normal, but she has never had the lived experience of the average Nigerian. Meanwhile, he does have that experience in his distant past, so he is able to relate to Ugwu and to understand what is natural in the village. Ultimately, however, he believes in modernizing and changing to the western paradigm for advancement. Thus, he questions Olanna's connection to the average Nigerian when he says, "You wouldn't know about things like that," but he is not able to make her see her folly, correct her ignorance, or push her outside of her Western comfort zone. In the meantime, Ugwu now smells like a woman, unlike his own people, and unlike men in the West. By Olanna's agency, he becomes an object of ridicule, but in his efforts to assimilate, he actually embraces this new way of life and rejects the old.

The trip that Ugwu and Odenigbo take to Opi to get Ugwu's sick mother illustrates this movement toward Western ways, for "Ugwu suddenly wished that Master would not touch his mother because her clothes smelled of age and must" (*HY*, 113). Thus, his new sensitivity to body odor and ordinary village smells leads him to think not of his mother's health but of the offensive smell of her clothing. He begins a partial rejection of the indigenous in favor of the new Western models offered by his neocolonial Igbo masters on Odim Street. When his mother asks about the nauseating smell coming from Odenigbo's and Olanna's mouths, he answers proudly, "Oh. That is toothpaste. We use it to clean our teeth," but his mother, who is not impressed, answers, "What is wrong with using a good *atu*? That smell has made me want to vomit" (116). Thus, she discredits his attempt to be Western with her own preference for the indigenous chewing stick. It is in this manner that Ugwu allows his mind to be colonized by the idealized Western manner of doing things and living life even as he yearns for a syncretism so that "he could join in the moonlight conversations and quarrels and yet live in Master's house with its running taps and refrigerator and stove" (117).

It is Ugwu's participation in the Biafran War, however, that really yields a definite move toward privileging indigenous knowledges, but only after he has experienced multiple roles in Nigerian society, moved from victim to victimizer, and reinserted into civil society. Ugwu starts the novel as a village boy, then a house servant, a starving and persecuted civilian wanted for combat, a drafted unwilling soldier, an abusive willing victimizer in the Biafran army, and, finally, an ex-combatant reinserting into civil society. As a village boy, Ugwu had been nurtured by his family's love and his own community's indigenous knowledge. When he arrives in Odim Street, however, he is awed by the Western lifestyle of his Igbo master and mistress, who make a concerted effort to fashion his existence after theirs even as they take full advantage of his labor for their own convenience. He is assimilated to a great extent during this period, for he lives a privileged life as a civilian and a student even as he serves as a houseboy.

Once the family leaves Nsukka and the Biafran army begins to lose the war, however, he slowly shifts into a victimized civilian. He is still the servant to the family but is now underfed, confined to avoid army conscription, and keenly aware of the plight of the average Igbo man and woman during the war. In Umuahia, he experiences bombings, builds a bunker, lives with rationed food sources, and becomes acquainted with life during war. In these circumstances of poor housing, scarce rations, and threatened lives, he understands the vulnerability of his master and mistress when not able to access the privilege that they have in Nsukka. However, he also understands his own mortality, Biafra's vulnerability to foreign powers, and his family's vulnerable position. Thus, he focuses on his relationship with his employers and Eberechi because he is so far away from his own kin.

The narrator captures Ugwu's fears and restrictions in a series of statements: "Ugwu hated the relief food" (*HT*, 355); "she no longer allowed him out during the day. Stories of forced conscription were everywhere" (356); and "images of his mother and Anulika and Nnesinachi splayed out underneath a dirty sun-blackened Hausa soldier came to Ugwu so clearly that he shivered" (358). Ugwu is no longer faced with the Western ideals of daily life that preoccupied the household in Odim Street; instead, he is faced with the daily survival struggle as he and his employers are forced to move to poorer housing, deal with malnutrition, and face losing the war. It is this struggle, combined with the disappointment of the insider knowledge he gains as a member of the Biafran army, that eventually moves him to reject Western paradigms of thinking.

Ugwu also has the problem of conscription, for it is forced upon him twice. The first time that he is captured and lined up with the other "recruits," Olanna gives the recruiter all their money so that Ugwu will be freed. Easily bribed, the army releases him. Olanna then chastises Ugwu, who suffers multiple assaults because he cannot move freely in his own country, he is being assaulted by the Biafran army recruiters, and he is responsible for the family's diminished resources because of the bribe to the recruiter. Shortly after the first thwarted recruitment, he is captured again and forced into service for the Biafran army, where "the casual cruelty of this new world in which he had no say grew a hard clot of fear inside him" (*HY*, 450). Unlike the Odim Street experience in which he also had very little say but was in service by choice, this is worse because he has absolutely no say in his actions since they are mandated by military training and by his commander. Thus, the army betrays him because "the people or institutions we depend on for survival violate us."[21] In Ugwu's case, the Biafran military forcefully separates him from his master's family and forces him to join in the fight for Biafra.

Furthermore, he faces great disappointment in this tattered army of conscripted soldiers, in which only one grand officer has a uniform, regular food, women, and all the other comforts. He also discovers that Biafra's most stellar weapon, the Ojukwu Bucket, is simply "a dull metal container full of scrap metal" (*HY*, 451), but the propaganda has made it seem as if it is the latest high-tech warfare gadget. This, he realizes, also holds for the descriptions of the Biafran army, which is not a collection of brave young men seeking freedom and emancipation from a hegemonic Nigeria, but rather a band of tattered conscripted soldiers who function without any restrictions and do as they please once assigned a mission. Thus, Ugwu "wished he could tell Eberechi about his disappointment," because "Ugwu's fear [had once] mixed with excitement at the thought that he was a soldier fighting for Biafra" (451). Now, however, he dissociates from his fellow freedom fighters because he no longer believes in the army as a fine-tuned war machine: "He did not want to know their stories. It was better to leave each man's load unopened, undisturbed, in his own mind" (453). However, in the course of fighting, he becomes rather entangled with High-Tech as a companion and accomplice in their abusive shenanigans.

Ugwu also takes on the name of "Target Destroyer" and the role of victimizer against the "bloody civilians" the Biafran army is supposed to be defending and liberating (*HY*, 455). For Ugwu and the civilians he abuses during his time in the army, "the core issue is betrayal—a betrayal of trust that produces conflict between external reality and a necessary system of social dependence."[22] Biafrans were being starved during the three-year civil war, and they simply cannot survive unless the Biafran army actually strives to conquer their independence. The random organization of the army renders its fighters just as dangerous for the average Biafran civilian, who is cursed and abused without provocation, as they are for the Nigerian. For instance, as previously described, forced conscriptions are daily business, corruption and bribery are an everyday occurrence, and the army is able to appropriate anything it says it needs for an operation regardless of its actual need or veracity. Thus, Target Destroyer's group hijacks a VW Beetle for a ride to the bar from an older couple, but only after humiliating them, beating them, and disregarding their admonishment of "This is wrong, officers. You have no right to take this car. I have my pass. I am working for our government" (456). The violence and chaos that are the norm during this war are dehumanizing for the Biafran civilians, who are victimized by international sanctions, Nigerian warfare, the Biafran army, and political and administrative corruption and incompetence.

The violence and chaos are also traumatic for the Biafran soldiers, who turn from victims to victimizers and thus betray the civilians just as they have been betrayed by the propaganda of the Biafran army. In Ugwu's case, the conscription is a betrayal, for he does not wish to fight in a war. He would rather help build refugee camps and help in the civilian efforts to support the war, but the threat of conscription kept him and many others from fully engaging in these behaviors that would have created an infrastructure of support for the army's efforts. Furthermore, the conscription of a child, an elderly man, and the disrespectful treatment that they receive at the hands of the child soldiers is also an affront to the village boy who believed in peaceful childhoods and family and village life. Thus, the Biafran army seems to betray Ugwu to such an extent that he becomes disillusioned with the cause and with the great war for Biafra.

The goat incident with the commander only reinforces the betrayal of the Igbo people by the politicians and by the corrupt officials of the army who take advantage of everyone they can. Ugwu has no choice in his recruitment, so he is helpless in the position of a "bloody civilian." He takes on the challenge of his conscription by striving to do well as a freedom fighter, for "he had proved himself to the other men by how well he did at training, how he scaled the obstacles and shimmied up the rough rope" (*HY*, 453). Instead of remaining a victim in this situation without a say over his future, Ugwu decides to take on the role of the strong man in the army. Thus, he goes along with his new comrades for the sake of fitting into this group and gaining some recognition and some agency, even as he victimizes average civilians, who are as helpless as he was before his conscription.

The gang rape of the bar girl is the quintessential experience of this role as victim turned victimizer. While initially Ugwu had actually stopped his group from harassing the server, he is eventually a participant in the gang rape of the girl who has done nothing but serve them properly. While High-Tech is the first to assault her, his comrades urge him to go next: "Target Destroyer is next!" and "*Ujo abiala o!* Target Destroyer is afraid!" . . . "The food is still fresh! Target Destroyer, aren't you a man? *I bukwa nwoke?*" (*HY*, 458). He gives in without much resistance and sexually assaults the young girl. The narrator tells us that he was "surprised at the swiftness of his erection. . . . He did not look at her face . . . he moved quickly and felt his own climax, the rush of fluids to the tips of himself: a self-loathing release" (458).

It is only after the assault that he looked at the girl and "she stared back at him with a calm hate" (*HY*, 458). She is the one for whom the Biafran army fights. It is for her freedom that they engage in this war, but the chaos of conflict has caused a change in these soldiers so that they transform from victims into victimizers even as they pretend to fight for freedom and independence and all things honorable for the Igbo. The girl is an Igbo villager, the very person they are supposed to protect and liberate. However, they victimize her so that they can feel their own power. In other words, their traumatic assaults on fellow Igbo people indicate a need to soothe themselves, gaining control through violence.

Adichie responds with Alice's words: "This is nonsense. We cannot keep beating people just because Nigeria is beating us" (*HY*, 474). Alice's words reveal that the victimized have, indeed, suddenly become victimizers because they can no longer tolerate their own status as victims. However, these Biafrans betray the greater Biafran population that is suffering to stay in solidarity with the Biafran army, which is purportedly fighting for freedom. Thus, it is their responsibility to strive to right the injustices of the Nigerian state. That is why the people chose secession: a Biafran war for independence. The accusations against the "bloody civilians" are without foundation. They serve only to identify scapegoats for Biafra's frustration at the deprivation and the imminent loss of the war.

Furthermore, Ugwu continues on his journey of development in the army, where he is wounded and finally rescued and brought to Olanna and Kainene's household. Once there, in the midst of a caring family, he begins to understand both his own trauma and that which he has caused others. Thus, when Richard picks him up at the hospital and tells him that he is writing a book titled *The World Was Silent When We Died*, he admits his flashbacks to the rape and his understanding of his own crime when the narrator states, "It haunted him, filled him with shame. It made him think about that girl in the bar, her pinched face and the hate in her eyes as she lay on her back on the dirty floor" (*HY*, 496).

In addition, while working as a teacher at the refugee camp, he learns of a priest's sexual abuse of the young starving girls, and he immediately contextualizes his own gang rape of the bar girl within this situation. Thus, he says, "Ugwu felt stained and unworthy. . . . He wondered what Kainene would say, what she would do to him, feel about him, if she ever knew about the girl in the bar. She would loathe him. So would Olanna. So would Eberechi" (*HY*, 499). His own understanding of his crimes while in the army is deeper as he reexperiences the depth of civilian deprivation and the love of freedom the Igbo people, his own people, hold so dear.

Given his immediate experience as one of "our boys" in the Biafran army, Ugwu dissociates from the reports on Radio Biafra and from the misleading hope and the happy propagandistic picture they painted. "Ugwu would get up and walk away. The shabby theatrics of the war reports, the voice that forced morsels of invented hope down people's throats, did not interest him" (*HY*, 500), because he knew that the fancy Ujukwu Buckets were simply buckets full of scrap metal and that the war was not going to be won by these men who wreaked as much havoc on the Igbo people as the Nigerians could. This scene also indicates his emotional numbness regarding the war. He is ready to live life, to connect to his indigenous life, and to reject the Western narrative of Biafran and Nigerian life. Thus, although Richard assures him that the speech from His Excellency "will be a great speech," Ugwu responds curtly yet knowingly, "There is no such thing as greatness" (500). He is painfully aware of the propaganda machine, and he has been part of the supposedly glorious messianic army. Therefore, he has no hope for Biafra.

Without hope for the Biafran cause, Ugwu turns to writing. Richard "admired Ugwu's ambition and his scribbling on any paper he could find. Once he had tried to find where Ugwu left some of them so he could take a look, but he had found none. They were probably all tucked into his shorts" (*HY*, 508). Later, Olanna sees him writing as well: "Ugwu was sitting on a bench writing" (511). However, he still participates in his daily home life and does not allow himself to dissociate from it as he has from the war. Instead, he is now tightly connected to this family as a member and not simply a servant.

In an effort to understand the many experiences in Biafra, he asks Olanna to tell him about the beginning of the war and her experience there. He also asks specifically about the child on the train whose severed head her mother carried lovingly in a calabash:

> Olanna was surprised, at first, by the question and then she realized that she clearly remembered how it was plaited and she began to describe the hairstyle, how some of the braids fell across the forehead. Then she described the head itself, the open eyes, the graying skin. Ugwu was writing as she spoke, and his writing, the earnestness of his interest, suddenly made her story important, made it serve a larger purpose that even she was not sure of, and so she told him all she remembered about the train full of people. (*HY*, 512)

Ogwu is collecting oral histories or witness testimony about the indigenous experience of the Biafran War, and given his own background, he focuses on the Igbo experience. This is the only knowledge that he can focus on: indigenous knowledge of the war. Richard is unequipped to really understand Nigeria or the Igbo because he is an outsider. Even through the Biafran War, as a British man, he has lived in relative comfort without living the many traumatic lives that Ugwu has been able to experience since the time he left his village to be a houseboy in a university professor's home.

When the news of an armistice and the end of the war reaches him, Ugwu is unable to feel anything because he is too privy to the inside knowledge of the devastation of the war and the flawed characters of fighters and civilians on both sides. His response to the announcement demonstrates his dissociation and his emotional numbing: "'What now, mah?' Ugwu asked, expressionless" (*HY*, 515). He is emotional about his return to see his family, for "it thrilled and frightened him, the thought that he would see Anulika in a few hours, that he would finally go home" (523). Thus, he feels reconnected to his own people by his experiences in the war, and he looks to them for nurturing and support. When he arrives, he is immediately grounded in the indigenous cosmology, for he must endure his family throwing sand at him and rubbing his body in disbelief to ensure that he is not a ghost.

He then learns of his mother's death from natural causes and has to physically prostrate himself on the grave to absorb her death. It is a reconnection with the land and the lessons of the woman who gave him birth as much as it is an understanding of his mother's death. Furthermore, he begins to understand the complexity of indigenous lives when he encounters Nnesinachi and learns of her agency in keeping his family alive through her relations with a Hausa soldier. While he had only ever conceived of her as an object of his desire without agency, will, or usefulness other than his penetration, he learns quickly that she is an Igbo woman, a subject and not simply the object of his fantasies, and the savior of his family. He also learns of his sister's being gang-raped and her physical maiming by five Nigerian soldiers, which closely parallels his own gang-rape of the bar girl. When he visited the stream, the place of the attack, "he sat down on a rock and sobbed" (*HY*, 526). It is not only in flashbacks that the memory of his traumatic assault haunts him but also in the lived realities of his sister's existence.

The end of the novel signals Adichie's turn to indigenous knowledges and a turn away from the Western paradigms of the knowledge depicted early in the novel. Thus, Richard praises Ugwu's writing as "fantastic" and asks him about it. Ugwu responds, "Yes, sah. It will be a part of a big book. It will take me many more years to finish it and I will call it 'Narrative of the Life of a Country'" (*HY*, 530). This is the book based on indigenous knowledges of lived life in Nigeria that must be written, and when Ugwu politely inquires about Richard's project, the latter responds, "The war isn't my story to tell, really," and "Ugwu nodded. He had never thought that it was" (531). Thus,

Ugwu's lived experience as an indigenous man living different realities, from that of a houseboy to a Biafran army soldier to a defeated civilian, renders him immeasurably more qualified and attuned to the life and experiences that must inform the writing.

Additionally, writing about the Biafran War serves as detraumatization, for it allows people to tell their life stories. It also provides an indigenous perspective on the new Nigeria that will have to be forged after the war because memory must be preserved in this renegotiation and rebuilding of a nation. Ugwu's book, and therefore Adichie's novel, is consistent with Dulue Mbachu's comment: "The truth is that up till this day, the complete story of Biafra has not been told. You cannot talk about Nigeria without Biafra."[23] Thus, Ugwu, who keeps his Biafran flag folded in a pair of trousers, says to Olanna, who is burning her Biafran pounds, "You're burning memory" (*HY*, 539). He will not allow his own indigenous memory to die with Biafra because there is a greater purpose in rebuilding Nigeria. Unlike Olanna and all those Westernized indigenous people who have lost their indigenous roots, Ugwu is actually more connected to them by the experience of the war. Thus, Adichie's novel is "an attempt to understand the men who carry out its most egregious violence; however, her primary purpose remains . . . to heed the voice of the silent abused."[24] Ugwu's character clearly allows her to illustrate both.

Thus, in Ugwu's book, the indigenous is privileged; and his dedication, which is written last, reads, "*For Master, my good man*" (*HY*, 541). He is still able to acknowledge his master's service to him: "But for Odenigbo, Ugwu would never have learned to read, write, or challenge the injurious values he learns in school."[25] However, with these five words, Ugwu reverses the status quo and privileges lived indigenous reality, while Richard's British and Odenigbo's Western and postmodern views are sidelined by his careful choice of words.

Ugwu's return to the ancestral appreciation of human beings and their indigenous knowledges is a sign of hope, because, as Achebe posited, "then literature can have an important and profound positive effect as well, functioning as a kind of bountiful, nourishing matrix for a healthy developing psyche."[26] It is thus that writing about the Biafran War serves as detraumatization while it privileges indigenous knowledges and looks to these as a source of hope for Nigeria's problems. It will also serve to reconnect others to their indigenous roots because, in Kainene's words, "Chiamaka should see life as it is, *ejima m*" (*HY*, 487), and the child represents the new generation that will have to forge a more indigenous and interethnically connected Nigeria in the post-Biafran era.

Writing of the Biafran War, therefore, serves to detraumatize as these authors, fictional and actual, turn to their own indigenous knowledges as a source for healing the trauma of their nations, Biafra and Nigeria. This writing from the indigenous lived experience heals both the colonial PTSD and the betrayal trauma of postcolonial civil war experience. Adichie strengthens this recognition in an interview with *World Literature Today,* in which she indirectly states her focus on indigenous knowledge in writing *Half of a Yellow Sun:* "I find that many of the books written about that period are more interested in the larger and grander narratives than in the small things that make up day-to-day life. I very much want the reader to feel what Biafra was like for ordinary middle-class men and women."[27] This privileging of indigenous knowledge is the key to understanding the Biafran War and its effect on the vanquished as well as the winners in the post–civil war Nigeria that must be imagined.

Thus, while spiders, ordinary inhabitants of the nation, have been previously killed by British and Westernized indigenous peoples in Africa, they are allowed to live at the end of the novel. They stand for the new experiences in Nigeria, and Adichie illustrates the change by writing, "A spider clambered up his arm but he did not slap it away. The darkness was black, complete, and Ugwu imagined the spider's hairy legs, its surprise to find not cold underground soil but warm human flesh" (*HY,* 453). This warm flesh of lived experience is the basis of the rebuilding of Nigeria and its memory so that the indigenous people's knowledge and lived realities will not be slapped away as unimportant. It is precisely on this knowledge that Adichie builds her novel, and it is this knowledge that will detraumatize Nigeria and help the nation move beyond Western modernist and postmodernist conceptions.

In addition, it is the privileging of the indigenous knowledge, along with the use of writing, in this novel that leads Ugwu to the security we see at the end of the novel. His security is that of the "large black spider moving slowly in its web, as if uncaring of their presence and still secure that this was its home" (*HY,* 522). In other words, this is Ugwu's character's stance at the end of the novel, even as he continues to be surrounded by a variety of neocolonial Western influences to which he is now impervious because he feels secure in his indigeneity, and he knows that Nigeria is *his* home, a web of his own.

Notes

1. Chimamanda Ngozi Adichie, *Half of a Yellow Sun* (New York: Anchor, 2007). Hereafter cited in text as *HY*.

2. Dulue Mbachu, quoted in Senan Murray, "The New Face of Nigerian Literature?" BBC News, http://news.bbc.co.uk/2/hi/africa/6731387.stm.

3. Lisa S. Beall, "Post-Traumatic Stress Disorder: A Bibliographic Essay," *Choice* 34, no. 6 (1997): 918.

4. Lenore Terr, *Too Scared to Cry: Psychotic Trauma in Childhood* (New York: Basic Books, 1990), 8.

5. Judith L. Herman, *Trauma and Recovery: The Aftermath of Violence—from Domestic Abuse to Political Terror* (New York: Basic Books, 1992); Herman, interviewed by Harry Kreisler, "The Case of Trauma and Recovery: Conversation with Judith Herman, M.D." (Berkeley: Institute of International Studies, University of California, September 21, 2000), http://globetrotter.berkeley.edu/people/Herman/herman-con3.html.

6. Cathy Caruth, *Unclaimed Experience: Trauma, Narrative, and History* (Baltimore: Johns Hopkins University Press, 1996), 13.

7. Jennifer J. Freyd, "What Is Betrayal Trauma? What Is Betrayal Trauma Theory?" (University of Oregon, 2009), http://dynamic.uoregon.edu/~jjf/defineBT.html.

8. In "The Story Behind the Book" on her website, Adichie says, "Both my grandfathers were interesting men, both born in the early 1900s in British-controlled Igbo land, both determined to educate their children, both with a keen sense of humor, both proud. I know this from stories I have been told. Eight years before I was born, they died in Biafra as refugees after fleeing hometowns that had fallen to federal troops. I grew up in the shadow of Biafra." http://www.halfofayellowsun.com/content.php?page=tsbtb&n=5&f=2.

9. Caruth, *Unclaimed Experience*, 3.

10. Frantz Fanon, *Black Skin, White Masks* (New York: Grove, 1967).

11. Sandra L. Bloom, "Trauma Theory Abbreviated," in *Final Action Plan: A Coordinated Community-Based Response to Family Violence* (Attorney General of Pennsylvania's Family Violence Task Force, October 1999), 7.

12. Ibid., 9.

13. Tsenay Serequeberhan, *The Hermeneutics of African Philosophy: Horizon and Discourse* (New York: Routledge, 1994), 2.

14. Hussein Abdilahi Bulhan, *Frantz Fanon and the Psychology of Oppression* (New York: Plenum, 1985), 13.

15. Chinua Achebe, *Hopes and Impediments: Selected Essays, 1965–1987* (Oxford: Heinemann, 1988), 112.

16. Fanon, *Black Skin,* 100.

17. Bulhan, *Frantz Fanon,* 58.

18. Heather Hewett, "Coming of Age: Chimamanda Ngozi Adichie and the Voice of the Third Generation," *English in Africa* 32, no. 1 (May 2005): 79.

19. Aimé Césaire, *Notebook of a Return to the Native Land,* trans. and ed. Clayton Eshleman and Annette Smith (Middleton, CT: Wesleyan University Press, 2001).

20. Frantz Fanon, *The Wretched of the Earth* (London: Pluto, 1963).

21. Freyd, "What Is a Betrayal Trauma?"

22. Ibid.

23. Mbachu, quoted in Murray, "The New Face of Nigerian Literature."

24. Hewett, "Coming of Age," 85.

25. E. Frances White, "While the World Watched," *Women's Review of Books* 24, no. 3 (May–June 2007): 10.

26. Achebe, *Hopes and Impediments,* 116.

27. "Author Profile: Chimamanda Ngozi Adichie," *World Literature Today* 80, no. 2 (March–April 2006): 5.

Part II

Decolonizing Public Spheres:
Conflicts and Negotiations

The Emergent Self in South African Black Consciousness Literature and Discourse

T. Spreelin MacDonald

> *I am married to the struggle*
> *The struggle to be human*
> *But I have but one life.*
>
> —Vonani Bila

Submergence and emergence. Spectacle and self. This chapter seeks to historicize a set of assertions about the relationship between self-hood and *the public*[1] evident in South African cultural discourse since the Black Consciousness Movement of the 1970s. These assertions act as a conceptual framework, placing primary value on the continual need for the establishment of an autonomous consciousness, or self, in relation to the public sphere, which is cast as a zone of submersion, superficiality, and disempowered consciousness. Whether in its early manifestations underlying the Black Consciousness dialectical self-assertion against the powers of apartheid public life, in its later turn away from the "spectacle" of public protest toward "ordinary" individual creative autonomy in the theoretical writings of Njabulo Ndebele, or in the diverse contemporary works of postapartheid intellectuals and writers such as Vonani Bila, Lesego Rampolokeng, and Zakes Mda, South African Black Consciousness–inspired literature and cultural commentary have redeployed this framework time and again, asserting the autonomous consciousness of the self (however defined) against the domination of consciousness in public life.

The concept of self is fundamental to South African Black Consciousness philosophy.[2] Indeed, in the writings of the founder of Black Consciousness, Steve Biko (1946–1977), which were largely compiled in the 1978 volume *I Write What I Like*, the affirmation of the self as the collective consciousness of black South Africans takes center stage.[3] "The philosophy of Black Consciousness," Biko states, "expresses group pride and the determination by the blacks to rise and attain the envisaged self."[4] Elsewhere, Biko expounds on this assertion, stating,

> Briefly defined therefore, Black Consciousness is in essence the realisation by the black man of the need to rally together with his brothers around the cause of their operation—the blackness of their skin—and to operate as a group in order to rid themselves of the shackles that bind them to perpetual servitude. It seeks to demonstrate the lie that black is an aberration from the "normal" which is white. It is a manifestation of a new realisation that by seeking to run away from themselves and to emulate the white man, blacks are insulting the intelligence of whoever created them black. . . . We want to attain the envisioned self which is a free self.[5]

As expressed in this passage, Black Consciousness posits the primacy of a collective black self. Biko asserts that the relationship of the black self to the white public sphere is explainable by "the Hegelian theory of dialectic materialism," in which the black self needs to be realized and dialectically asserted as an antithesis of the thesis of white domination in order to realize a future in which an egalitarian South African society could be achieved as the synthesis of this dialectic.[6] Biko argues, "If South Africa is to be a land where black and white live together in harmony without fear of group exploitation, it is only when these two opposites have interplayed and produced a viable synthesis of ideas and a *modus vivendi*" that this synthesis will come about.[7]

While such a synthesis is an ultimate goal, the immediate imperatives of self-realization and group assertion are the most pressing because a synthesis is achievable, according to Biko, only by first extracting the self of the black group from its dominated position in the public life of apartheid. Black Consciousness can be rehabilitated and the black self can be posited only as an antithesis from a position of withdrawal.[8] Such an extraction is necessary because the present public sphere toward which Biko writes is one of aggressive apartheid racism, and also because it is one constituted by a form of domination Biko defines as more insidious than overt oppression: white liberalism. Liberals "are the greatest racists for they refuse to credit us with any intelligence to know what we want," Biko argues.[9] Biko identifies white liberalism as the greatest barrier to the achievement of Black Consciousness because it masks the structuring racism of public life behind a myth of universal equality, in which discourse alone is thought to bring about change. Feeding on such an illusion accordingly saps blacks' ability to realize their own consciousness, simultaneously offering a masked whiteness while diffusing a positive black self-consciousness. Of this liberalism, Biko states that

> while we progressively lose ourselves in a world of colour-lessness and amorphous common humanity, whites are deriving pleasure and security in entrenching white racism and further exploiting the minds and bodies of the unsuspecting black masses. Their agents are ever present amongst us, telling us that it is immoral to withdraw into a cocoon, that dialogue is the answer to our problem.[10]

According to Biko's conception, this form of public life, structured by the mediation of black needs by white liberal priorities and platitudes of dialogue, must be vigorously rejected. It is only in the "cocoon" of withdrawal that blacks will be able to find their consciousness, the self which they will need in order to transform their position and assert themselves dialectically against white domination. Yet, while Biko is certainly primarily concerned with the short-term achievement of black collective self and its subsequent assertion, his conception also leaves the door open for reinterpretations that prioritize other forms of selfhood, including that of individual self-consciousness over other forms of self-incorporation.[11] For instance, this space for the acknowledgment of individual consciousness is enabled when Biko states:

> At the heart of this kind of thinking is the realization by the blacks that the most potent weapon in the hands of the oppressor is the mind of the oppressed. . . . Hence thinking along lines of Black Consciousness makes the black man see himself as a being, entire in himself, and not as an extension of a broom or additional leverage to some machine. At the end of it all, he cannot tolerate attempts by anybody to dwarf the significance of his manhood.[12]

Such an exhortation effectively establishes ground on which to understand the rejection of psychological domination to be possible, even necessary, at the individual level. While the individual may define themselves as black, their particular consciousness, their individual self, is integral to, even of primary importance over, the realization of other levels of selfhood, for they must first of all recognize themselves as *not* the "extension" of some other unit of being. The individual consciousness is asserted as primary.

Biko's Black Consciousness undoubtedly saw the assertion of any identity to be, first of all, necessarily oriented toward the liberation of the black collective, yet the possibilities availed in such passages, which reject the domination by the self at the most basic individual level, establish a space in which subsequent theorists and artists have reinterpreted the terms of Black Consciousness selfhood, logically emphasizing the individual self at the heart of Black Consciousness discourse. No other example of such a reinterpretation is more apparent than Njabulo Ndebele's use of this framework to assert the necessary autonomy of the individual self as the vehicle for an "emergent" South African individual, group, and national freedom.[13] In what has come to be widely regarded as one of the seminal cultural commentaries of late apartheid and early democratic South Africa,[14] a series of essays collected and published in 1991 as *Rediscovery of the Ordinary: Essays on South African Literature and Culture*, Ndebele puts forth a critique of cultural production in the context of the "spectacle" of apartheid, stating,

> Everything in South Africa has been mind-bogglingly spectacular: the monstrous war machine developed over the years; the random massive pass raids; mass shootings and killings; mass economic exploitation, the ultimate symbol of which is the mining industry; the mass removals of people; the spate of draconian laws passed with the spectacle of parliamentary promulgations; the luxurious life-style of whites: servants, all encompassing privilege, swimming pools, and high commodity consumption; the sprawling monotony of architecture in African locations, which are the very picture of poverty and oppression. The symbols are all over: the quintessence of obscene social exhibitionism.[15]

Here, Ndebele represents public life in apartheid as a "spectacle," in that its brazen public "exhibitionism" pushes the limits of the imagination, threatening to exhaust individual autonomous consciousness.[16] As T. T. Moyana similarly observed, apartheid "life itself is too fantastic to be outstripped by the creative imagination."[17]

Yet, in a crucial shift from Biko's dialectics, Ndebele sees such anxiety not as being rooted in the failure of blacks to assert themselves collectively against white domination, but, rather, as produced by the failure to cultivate consciousness at the level of the individual autonomous self. Consciousness must first be developed through the recognition of the individual self as the bedrock of autonomy. Attempts to assert group self against white domination simply draw one into the "spectacle" of the dominating logic of the public realm in which consciousness is exhausted by the "protest" demands of action and reaction in an "absurd" exhibitionist spectacle of power relations.[18] In this context, individual self-consciousness is enfolded and flattened in cycles of reactionary protest. What's more, such anti-individuality is policed by the group for the sake of solidarity. As Ndebele states elsewhere, "The necessity of closing ranks meant the suppression of criticism, even if that criticism could strengthen the movement in the long run. In other words, the controls that the state imposed upon everyone, we imposed upon ourselves."[19]

To state the ramifications of this process more plainly in terms of artistic production, according to Ndebele, black South African art under apartheid is locked into a superficial cycle of "protest" works, which negate imagination and the representation of "causality" in such social drama, for the endless representation of "the spectacular contest between the powerless and the powerful."[20] Ndebele argues, "There is very little attempt to delve into intricacies of motive or social process. People and situations are either very good or very bad."[21] Quoting Roland Barthes, Ndebele equates such representation with the "absurd" desolation of individual consciousness, stating:

> What is on display here is the spectacle of social absurdity. The necessary ingredients of this display are precisely the triteness and barrenness of thought, the almost deliberate waste of intellectual energy on trivialities. It is, in fact, the "emptying out of interiority to the benefit of its exterior signs, [the] exhaustion of the content by the form." The overwhelming form is the method of displaying the culture of oppression to the utmost in bewilderment.[22]

Ndebele's assertion is that individual consciousness is relinquished when circumvented by placing black group self in simple dialectical opposition with whiteness. Such a practice assumes little other than that the logic of spectacular superficiality and consciousness loses its autonomy. It is key here that Ndebele rejects Biko's fundamentally dialectic vision of the self's relation to the public struggle while retaining the underlying concept of the necessary emergence of the self from public domination. That is, while atomizing the notion of the group self, he retains the conceptual notion that it is necessary for the self to be an emergent autonomous consciousness. Thus, Ndebele reinvents this foundational Black Consciousness notion of the need for the self to assert its autonomy and emerge from the domination of the public realm to validate a turn toward a prioritization of the individual consciousness. In so doing he proposes a *renascence* of sorts in the recovery of interiority in South African cultural production (most specifically, literature), one based on what he terms "the rediscovery of the ordinary," of which he states: "The ordinary is defined as the opposite of the spectacular. The ordinary is sobering rationality; it is the forcing of attention on necessary detail. Paying attention to the ordinary and its methods will result in a significant growth of consciousness."[23]

Crucial to Ndebele's reinvention of the Black Consciousness self is this assertion that "the rediscovery of the ordinary," which he identifies in a growing number of literary works, is itself an increasing trend. It is the beginning of a broader emergence of a revalidation of the innate human self through individual consciousness, the groundwork for a new civilization based upon a renascence in the representation of an always present, but long-neglected individual consciousness:

> Young writers appear to have taken up the challenge, albeit unwittingly. They seemed prepared to confront the human tragedy together with the immense challenging responsibility to create a new society. This demands an uncompromisingly tough-minded creative will to build a new civilisation. And no civilisation worth the name will emerge without the payment of disciplined and rigorous attention to detail.[24]

Such passages describe the emergence of the self of a civilization through the cultivation of the minute subjectivities of individual consciousness that have long been buried by the spectacle of collective oppression. Thus, in relation to the public sphere of its time, one dominated by Biko's notion of group dialectics, this essay asserts its reformation along the lines of a renascence, or rediscovery, of the autonomous individual self, which both breaks with Biko's group dialects and capitalizes on the underlying conceptual imperative of an emergent autonomous self-consciousness modeled in Biko's writing. With an understanding of both the vocabulary ("self," "ordinary," "spectacle," "emergence"), and the conceptual framework within which such terms are couched, one can begin to recognize the salience of notions of the Black Consciousness self in the contemporary field of literary and cultural discourse in South Africa. More crucially, one can also identify the manners in which the elasticity of this notion of the emergent autonomous self allows it to be continually reapplied in the public context of the postapartheid era.

The highly influential nature of the vocabulary that Ndebele infuses into representational practices of the self is evident in the lasting use of the terms "ordinary" and "spectacle" among South African artists in articulating their work. Consider very recent statements by two of South Africa's most prominent and influential writers, Zakes Mda and Lesego Rampolokeng. In an interview with a regional television station in the United States during a 2007 book tour, Mda was asked if he felt at home in Athens, Ohio, where he has lived for the past several years as a professor of creative writing. Mda responded that he is not entirely at home anywhere, elaborating that

> even in South Africa I'm both a stranger and at home. It is the same in Athens, Ohio. I live in Athens, Ohio. My family is there, you know. I have a house there, which makes it home. But, still, I mean, I'm an outsider, you see. And I prefer it that way, because as an outsider *I'm able to rediscover the ordinary*. I'm able to look at things with a fresh eye, with a new eye, you know.[25]

Here, Mda articulates his position as an artist in South Africa and abroad strongly in terms of Ndebele's interpretation of Black Consciousness selfhood. He asserts the duty of the artist to maintain distance from the whole in order to produce detailed, "ordinary," and "fresh" representations enabled by an autonomous individual consciousness. Mda views himself as an intentionally extracted outsider, one who gains his identity through his autonomy in relation to any "home." He universally defines his identity, then, as one of a necessary individual self-consciousness, unbound by place or expected affiliations, which allows him to engage in this continual renascence, or "rediscovery of the ordinary."

A second marker of the strong residual influence of Ndebele's updating of the conceptual framework of Black Consciousness selfhood comes in a feature article in South Africa's *Mail & Guardian* news-paper about the poet and dramaturge Lesego Rampolokeng and his new play, *Bantu Ghost: A Stream of (Black) Unconsciousness*. The article begins,

> Ask poet Lesego Rampolokeng where he has been for the past few years and he'll tell you that he was avoiding "*the spectacle*" that poetry gatherings have become. "I went to a few so-called events and I was struck by the uniformity of the whole thing. . . . So I said I wasn't going to be a part of that. I didn't want to be monkey dancing anymore."[26]

While Mda states that his autonomy allows for the emergence of creations from the perspective of "a new eye," Rampolokeng simi-larly, and with his characteristic stringency, balks at the superficiality ("'spectacle'") and coercion ("'monkey dancing'") of public life. Rather than being co-opted into the public spectacle, Rampolokeng envisions his reengagement (somewhat in Biko's dialectic terms, yet at the indi-vidual level) with the public sphere from a position of a consolidated, individual, autonomous selfhood. Thus, Rampolokeng states:

> I just wasn't going out and advertising myself because you get neutralised by applause. . . . Like when you get paid to scream and shout and be "militant." I came out [not because of the need for applause but] because there were issues that I felt strongly enough about expressing and I believed that I could express them, in a way that was true to me and to me alone.[27]

Here, Rampolokeng characterizes the public sphere as a zone in which autonomous self-consciousness is "neutralised" by applause, and (á la Ndebele's critique of protest works) "militancy" is super-ficial and bound up in power relations. It is a space in which one's self-consciousness is disempowered, hence the name of Rampolo-keng's new play, *Bantu Ghost: A Stream of (Black) Unconsciousness*.[28] The public of postapartheid South Africa is thus seen to be inhabited by the ghost of Steve Biko and black South Africa's killed conscious-ness. Accordingly, Rampolokeng expresses a need to disengage, to continually reemerge, for his consciousness to engage in a *renascence* of its possible autonomy, and the imperative of not being coerced into public "unconsciousness."

The manner in which Rampolokeng characterizes his own intellectual genealogy expresses much of this conceptual framework and its Black Consciousness lineage: "Throughout my life I have always been inspired by certain people who have just never sold out their vision, who would much rather be ignored or battered down by whoever wields the power to do so." . . . The "deviants," as he calls them, "the militants who fell off the conveyor belt," form a sprawling roll call of black thinkers that includes the likes of Mafika Gwala, Steve Biko, and Amiri Baraka.[29]

Such discourse strongly affirms the conceptual links between Biko's *I Write What I Like,* Ndebele's *Rediscovery of the Ordinary,* and the reflexive self-commentary of these two prominent contemporary artists. Imagining the necessity of striving for the status of the "stranger," "deviant" self is enabled by this underlying bulwark of the emergent autonomous self as an imperative to consciousness and creativity.

Yet, this conceptual framework should not be seen as inhabiting cultural discourse alone. One of the richest contemporary reinventions of this framework comes in the poetry of Vonani Bila, a rural-based poet who writes in Xitsonga, English, Sepedi, and a number of other languages, and is the founder and director of the Timbila Poetry Project, a movement that seeks to cultivate contemporary black South African development through the arts.[30]

Robert Berold, the founding editor of South Africa's preeminent poetry journal *New Coin,* has remarked that "Bila's work comes out of the expansive aesthetic of black consciousness performance poetry full of outrage, declamation and accusation."[31] Indeed, much of the poetry in Bila's four major collections—*No Free Sleeping* (1998, with Donald Parenzee and Alan Finlay); *In the Name of Amandla* (2005); *Magicstan Fires* (2006); and *Handsome Jita* (2007)—does engage in a spirit of "declamation," which can be alternatively embraced as rooted in the ethic of Black Consciousness dialectics, or dismissed, in Ndebele's terms, as mere works of "protest." But neither interpretation is descriptive of the depth and sensitivity of Bila's appropriation of the fundamental motif of Black Consciousness literature, the concept of the autonomous self; nor do they account for his crucial reinvention of the terms in which this notion is applied. Consider, for instance, portions of Bila's 2005 poem "Comrade." The first stanza of the poem reads,

Comrade, don't drag me to endless meetings
To protest the capitalist
Fight the smug elites
Be it in Washington, Seattle
Geneva or Davos
We never act
Nor reach any resolution

This stanza introduces and historicizes the position of the public function of the demonstrator, and expresses exhaustion in the ineffectiveness of public dialectic relationships, somewhat in line with both Ndebele's critique and Rampolokeng's exasperation at the practice of "monkey dancing." The poem proceeds in the third stanza to locate such ill will toward this public protest function in the desire for another form of individual, private consciousness:

Comrade, age is catching up with me
I look around you, my mentors
You are all well divorced
Loneliness eats my heart away
I have no wife
No child

The speaker is nagged by the private toll of a public life in which bonds of public demonstration (camaraderie) are parasitic on those of private intimacy (family). In the fourth stanza, the speaker beseeches his comrade,

I want to take my girl to a cinema
Go on a romantic walk at the Durban beach
. . . .
I want to climb the mountain, her cheering me
I want to take her to dinner so we could go home
Make love
Make a home.

This speaker's desire for intimate applause, the applause of a loved one exalting one's private feats, is comparable to Rampolokeng's rejection of the numbing, neutralizing effect of public applause. Private applause is in line with the needs of a private level of consciousness. The other form of applause is public, superficial, and a function of the power of the public to dominate consciousness through praise.

In this private sense, "Comrade" expresses the fundamental Black Consciousness need to seek an emergent self, and to distance that self from public domination. Yet, in key ways, "Comrade" expresses a new application of this concept. In an original turn, Bila's speaker does not prioritize the group, individual, or national levels of selfhood evident in previous applications of this concept. Rather, he develops a level of intimate familial relationships as the primary site of the self. The allegiance of his speaker to his "comrade" and their group function is insufficient. So, too, is individuality, as is evident in the negativity associated with the divorced status of his comrades. The self that needs to emerge in this new use is the self of the family unit. It is the private autonomy of the family over the group, nation, or "stranger"/"deviant" selves of the other influential strands of this discourse.

While not establishing Bila's as the final word in the process of reinventing the Black Consciousness concept of the emergent autonomous self, his poetry serves as a rich example of the continual potency of this conception in articulating the changing ideologies of the self of the past thirty years of Black Consciousness discourse and literature. At its essence, Black Consciousness asserts the autonomy of self. While established in *I Write What I Like* as a foundational concept, this autonomy is not bound by the group dialectics toward which Biko lends it.

In fundamentally asserting the broadly interpretable notion of the need for a continually emergent autonomous self, Black Consciousness leaves the door open for reinterpretation of the hierarchy of incorporation in which self must be invoked. Thus, subsequent waves of Black Consciousness thinkers have taken the assertion of autonomous self to the individual, group, and family levels, with the national self all the while lurking as the future self. Ultimately, the productive element of Black Consciousness in such literature and discourse is its validation of the continual need for self-assertion, however the self may be defined.

Notes

1. As "the public" is subject to a wide number of definitions, I refer here to Michael Warner's definition: "*The* public is a kind of social totality. Its most common sense is that of the people in general. It might be

people organized as the nation, the commonwealth, the city, the state, or some other community. It might be very general, as in Christendom or humanity. But in each case, the public, as a people, is thought to include everyone within the field in question. This sense of totality is brought out by speaking of *the* public." Michael Warner, *Publics and Counterpublics* (Brooklyn: Zone Books, 2002), 65.

2. There is an important distinction to be made here between the *South African* Black Consciousness exclusively addressed in this chapter and the Black Consciousness of the United States, which were both conceived in roughly the same period of the 1960s. While the movements certainly drew on some of the same sources of inspiration, such as the writings of Frantz Fanon (especially *Black Skin, White Masks* [New York: Grove Press, 1967]; and *The Wretched of the Earth* [London: Pluto, 1963]), and created some transatlantic cross-fertilization of thought with each other, they also developed in some distinct manners and contexts, not least among these being their varied reactions to a number of different linguistic, cultural, and political factors (Jacques Louw, "Journalism and the Law," in *Changing the Fourth Estate: Essays on South African Journalism*, ed. Adrian Hadland [Cape Town: HSRC Press, 2005], 127; Thomas K. Ranuga, 182–91).

3. Steve Biko, *I Write What I Like* (London: Bowerdean Press, 1978; Chicago: University of Chicago Press, 2002). All citations refer to the Chicago Press edition. While Biko was certainly the central charismatic leader of Black Consciousness and has subsequently taken on iconic status as its martyr since his assassination in 1977, several other black intellectuals were central to the intellectual conception of the movement, including Mamphela Ramphele, Barney Pityana, Charles Sibisi, Mandla Langa, Strini Moodley, and Saths Cooper (Louw, "Journalism and the Law," 124; see also Mamphela Ramphele, *Across Boundaries: The Journey of a South African Woman Leader* [New York: Feminist Press, 1996]).

4. Biko, *I Write What I Like*, 68.

5. Ibid., 49. Though *I Write What I Like* was originally written and published in English, scholars often render the word "operation" as "oppression" when quoting this passage (see Duncan Brown, *Voicing the Text: South African Oral Poetry and Performance* [Cape Town: Oxford University Press, 1998], 169). I have been unable to establish the citational history that allowed for this divergence.

6. Ibid., 51.

7. Ibid.

8. Ibid.

9. Ibid.

10. Ibid., 50. It could also be argued that Biko does not envision blackness as distinguishable from any element of identity, be that individual, group, or national, since he argues that the eventual nation will be black in its identity and priorities, as well (Louw, "Journalism and the Law," 128). The point of distinction I make here is not about the racial aspects of these various levels of identity, but rather about the different natures of incorporation that each entails. The assertion of the individual self against the group is therefore primarily an assertion of autonomy from a form of incorporation, more than it is a shedding of racial identity.

11. Biko, *I Write What I Like*, 68.

12. Ibid.

13. Anthony O'Brien, "Njabulo Ndebele and Radical Democratic Culture," in *Against Normalization: Writing Radical Democracy in South Africa* (Durham, NC: Duke University Press, 2001), 36–75. Tony Morphet compares Ndebele's assertions with those of another seminal statement of the late apartheid phase, Albie Sachs's essay "Preparing Ourselves for Freedom," which made similar revisionist cultural demands. Morphet states that both positions share a "redemptive" emphasis, in the sense that they urge the process of "break[ing] free from the solemn formulas of commitment" (Sachs, 3), or "break[ing] down the closed epistemological structures of South African oppression" (Ndebele, 45; Morphet, 95).

14. O'Brien, *Against Normalization*, 37.

15. Njabulo S. Ndebele, *Rediscovery of the Ordinary: Essays on South African Literature and Culture* (Scottsville, South Africa: University of Kwa-Zulu–Natal Press, 2006), 31–32. First edition published 1991 by the Congress of South African Writers.

16. Ibid., 31–53.

17. T. T. Moyana, "Problems of a Creative Writer in South Africa," in *Aspects of South African Literature*, ed. Christopher Heywood (London: Heinemann, 1976), 95.

18. For this framing, I am indebted to Michael Warner's discussion of public-counterpublic relations in *Publics and Counterpublics*, 124.

19. Njabulo Ndebele, quoted in Duncan Brown, *Voicing the Text: South African Oral Poetry and Performance* (Cape Town: Oxford University Press, 1998).

20. Ndebele, *Rediscovery of the Ordinary*, 33, 38.

21. Ibid., 33.

22. Ibid., 33. Bracketed portion of quote is from Roland Barthes, *Mythologies*, trans. Annette Lavers (London: Jonathan Cape, 1972).

23. Ibid., 46. Susan Vanzanten Gallagher notes that such assertions by Ndebele strongly echo earlier indictments by Lewis Nkosi and more or less

contemporary observations by J. M. Coetzee about the poverty of protest literate and the need for a new mode of experimental creativity. Gallagher, "The Backward Glance: History and the Novel in Post-Apartheid South Africa," *Studies in the Novel* 29, no. 3 (1997): 380.

24. Ndebele, *Rediscovery of the Ordinary*, 53.

25. Zakes Mda, interview by Rob Caldwell, October 10, 2007, WCSH6, Portland, Maine, accessed October 23, 2007, emphasis added, http://www.wcsh6.com/news/article.aspx?storyid=72260.

26. Kwanele Sosibo, "No More Monkey Dancing," *Mail and Guardian Online,* accessed October 12, 2007, emphasis added, www.chico.mweb/co.za/art/2007/2007oct/071012-lesego.html.

27. Ibid. The words in brackets are original to Lesego Rampolokeng, *Bantu Ghost: A Stream of (Black) Unconsciousness* (Johannesburg: Market Theatre Laboratory, 2007).

28. Steve Biko's middle name was "Bantu," and "bantu" has historically (especially during apartheid) been used to label black Africans as a people in South Africa and beyond.

29. From Sosibo, "No More Monkey Dancing." Gwala is a South African Black Consciousness poet who was prominent largely in the 1970s and 1980s. Baraka is an African American poet central to American Black Consciousness since the 1960s. The poster advertisement for *Bantu Ghost: A Stream of (Black) Unconsciousness* lists a number of other prominent African and diasporic black artists and intellectuals, including Fanon and his fellow Martinican Aimé Césaire; as well as the Congo's first president, Patrice Lumumba; the African American poet Sonia Sanchez; and several other figures.

30. Vonani Bila, *Magicstan Fires* (Elim, South Africa: Timbila, 2006).

31. Vonani Bila, *In the Name of Amandla* (Elim, South Africa: Timbila, 2005).

The Public Life of Reason

Orchestrating Debate in Postapartheid South Africa
Lesley Cowling and Carolyn Hamilton

The notion that intellectuals have a role to play in social processes customarily draws on Enlightenment ideas that privilege critical rationality as central to the operations of society. In this conception, the use of reason is not confined to experts or educationists in their places of work, but is fundamental to public life. For Kant, the public use of reason was a basic right of citizens in a democratic order. Splichal reminds us of Kant's (and, generally, the Enlightenment's) belief that "citizens must be convinced by reason in the exercise of public debate that public policies are just, otherwise the state loses its moral legitimacy."[1] This principle underpins many of the normative understandings of how democracies and their component structures should function. The idea of publicness was developed more recently by Jurgen Habermas, who drew on a historical account of the Enlightenment concepts of reason and the public to further delineate the public sphere as a space between the people and the state, in which individuals come together to debate, in a rational critical fashion, issues of common interest to society.[2]

In such a conception of public deliberation, intellectuals and expert commentators are seen to play a crucial role by representing various positions in a debate and critically engaging with the issues. They are also assumed to bring specialist knowledge or complexity to the discussion. While intellectuals are often defined as members of a learned intelligentsia, popular thinkers drawing on grassroots experiences who engage with pertinent issues in reflective and complex ways are also recognized. Gramsci spoke of all men as intellectuals, allowing for the existence of what he called "organic intellectuals," but he also observed that "not all men have in society the function of intellectuals."[3] Others have argued (notably Edward Said) that intellectuals, as thinkers who are independent of the state and other interests, have an obligation to "speak the truth to power."[4]

However, as Said points out, it is not a simple matter for an intellectual to step into the public domain. For citizens to engage in public debate, they need to have access to public platforms, such as the media. Entry to such arenas is controlled by gatekeepers who apply a range of criteria in admitting individuals, allowing them to speak and creating the conditions under which they can engage. Studies of journalism have shown that access to the media, in particular, is controlled and constrained by multiple gatekeeping practices.[5] Even if certain individuals are admitted to public debate through these arenas, they may not necessarily have control over their part in the debate and over the way in which it unfolds.

So, in considering the public role and responsibilities of intellectuals in society, we need to consider the context in which they operate: the ways in which certain individuals are authorized to speak and others are curtailed or excluded; the selection of issues for discussion; and the ways in which the dynamics of the debate operate. We draw from research on public debate in the media in South Africa to examine these questions,[6] reasoning that as well as being a key player in the production of debate, the media simultaneously function as a space in which debate takes place.

This chapter focuses on two key areas. It first examines the ongoing contestations over the definition of intellectuals, their roles, and the rules of public discussion—a debate about debate. Much of this contestation has found its way into the media, through reports and commentary, or been produced there. The second focus of the chapter concerns the values and practices of media gatekeepers involved in the production of debate, and their opposition by certain sectors in society, in particular, the ruling political party, the African National Congress (ANC). Our focus on these two areas establishes an ongoing contestation over the meaning of "the public," rooted in different intellectual inheritances, the legacies of the Enlightenment and of national democratic struggle, both strongly current in contemporary South Africa. Depending on how "the public" and "the public interest" are understood, the role of intellectuals in speaking in the public domain is differently conceptualized. These differences, we argue, underlie sharply divergent points of departure about the nature of public debate, which inform the question of who should speak, in what ways, and to what topics.

Background

South Africa is arguably Africa's newest postcolonial state, a society shaped by the transition from a racialized totalitarian regime to a constitutional democracy and a transnational free-market economy. Public deliberation is a marked feature of the governmental, civic, and public arrangements. In part, this is a consequence of the country's transition to democracy through a negotiated settlement, which agreed on a constitution enshrining individual rights, including freedom of expression. The culture of open and free public speech also flows from certain South African historical legacies that valorize deliberation. These include celebrated traditions of community discussions as well as forms of public engagement by African intellectuals that date back to at least the nineteenth century and a concern about the historical exclusion of the majority from the concept of the public itself. These various inherited legacies result in significant value being placed on popular participation in public deliberation today.

As Hamilton argues,[7] the value of public participation is currently institutionalized in a range of instruments, organizations, and policies, through which citizens are offered the opportunity to comment on government initiatives and other issues of public concern. The South African Constitution, and its extrapolation into law by the Constitutional Court, lays a responsibility to be transparent and accountable on the executive, and an obligation on the legislature to facilitate public involvement in its proposed legislation. The Constitutional Court has made it clear that South African democracy is not only representative, but in fact contains participatory elements, viz., participation by the public on a continual basis and active involvement by citizens in public affairs.[8]

The importance of public deliberation is also underpinned in the Constitution through its provision for freedom of expression, enshrined in the Bill of Rights. The media are recognized in judicial rulings as the bearers of this value,[9] and have been able to rely upon it to their advantage in postconstitutional legal disputes. There have been substantial efforts geared toward the stimulation of public deliberation on public television and radio. The coverage of the Truth and

Reconciliation Commission by the South African public broadcaster SABC, for example, was consciously intended to provoke a national reflection on the brutalities of the apartheid state and the role of certain individuals and organizations in oppression.[10] There have been a number of issue-driven talk shows on television, too, geared toward reflecting on South Africa's transition to a democratic state. Considerable attention has been given to creating participation in ideas and issues in the public sphere through a range of television and radio programming, either through the medium of talk or through educational programs intended to prompt deliberation.[11]

The Mbeki presidency of 1999–2008 engaged in intensive monthly face-to-face consultations with communities. In addition, individuals on the president's staff participated actively in public engagement by writing opinion pieces for the commercial media, the Internet, and publishing books and articles.[12]

Thabo Mbeki was characterized as an intellectual, not only by his peers in the ruling party, but by the local and international media, including the *New Statesman*, the *Guardian*, the *Economist*, and the *New York Times*.

He wrote a regular letter on the African National Congress website, addressing a range of issues in an intellectual register, and this was routinely reported on by the South African media and discussed by a range of commentators. In this fashion, Mbeki became an agenda-setter for debate in the party and in the media, and stimulated reflection on a range of issues. One of these issues was the role of intellectuals, particularly black "African" intellectuals, and he repeatedly called for active engagement by black intellectuals in public deliberation. Another theme was the need for an "African Renaissance," a philosophy that underlay Mbeki's promotion of the New Partnership for Africa's Development (Nepad), "a vision and a framework for Africa's renewal."[13]

South Africa has thus been an environment that appears to be strongly enabling of public deliberation, and particularly hospitable to intellectuals and critique. It also appears to have vibrant, diverse, and untrammeled media. However, in the years of the Mbeki presidency, a series of controversies erupted around questions of who was entitled to speak, how they should speak, and what role the media were playing and should have been playing in the debate. Paradoxically, the upshot of these key public contests was the sense that intellectual deliberation was closing down.

The Intellectual Presidency

Many disputes about the nature of public engagement swirled around the figure of Thabo Mbeki, so it would be tempting to lay the responsibility for the hostilities at his door, as some commentators have done.[14] However, the contests have not ended, or become less antagonistic or less personalized, since he was deposed in 2008. Early in his first term, the Mbeki presidency's interventions in public deliberation generated disquiet in some quarters, as they were seen as not merely attempts to get the nation thinking about various issues, but attempts to silence and intimidate critics, in Hamilton's term, a "corralling" of deliberation.[15] Before Mbeki was openly challenged by factions within the ruling party in 2007, there was a concern that he was centralizing power in himself and his cabinet. As Chipkin notes:

> Thabo Mbeki's presidency was dogged by accusations of authoritarianism: that he was centralising political power in the Executive, eviscerating Parliament by reducing it to a "rubber stamp" role, blurring the lines between party and state, closing down opposition in the African National Congress (especially over Macro-Economic policy) itself and orchestrating the harsh rebuttal of dissenters in civil society (over HIV/AIDS, crime, lack of service delivery, corruption).[16]

Academic Sipho Seepe led the charge against this perceived corralling of debate in highly adversarial attacks on Mbeki in his column for the weekly *Mail & Guardian*, from 1999 to 2002. Zvomuya[17] notes that in his columns, Seepe referred to "an increased resort to name-calling and personal attacks on intellectuals, both black and white, who criticized government policies. The one group was dismissed as racist, whilst the other was branded as 'sellouts and lackeys of anti-transformation whites.'"[18] Seepe wrote of "malicious attacks against some of the country's best medical scientists, charges of racism, witch hunts and intellectual intimidation."[19] Much of his attack was directed at the ways in which the debate was conducted. He objected in particular to the tendency for arguments emanating from the presidency to be *ad hominem*, often using the marker of race to discredit speakers who raised issues, rather than engaging substantively with their arguments, and the discrediting was seen by Seepe (and others) as an expedient maneuver to deflect criticism.

However, it was not simply the stance of the proponents of the president's views that offended Seepe. Zvomuya argues that Seepe's persistent attacks on the "myth of the intellectual president" attest to Seepe's discomfort with the president's occupying the public space *as intellectual*, and "his underlying feeling that Mbeki is appropriating a centre that is not his";[20] in other words, he sees Mbeki as seeking to dominate the intellectual space. Zvomuya cites many examples of Seepe's distaste for political views being presented as intellectual argument, for example: "What is most strange in South Africa is that it is its politicians, a majority of whom have dubious educational qualifications and/or intellectual standing, if any, who have usurped the role of identifying and defining what constitutes an intellectual life."[21] Seepe, Zvomuya argues, is thus the intellectual "negotiating for space in the public arena where intellectual politicians are also negotiating for dominance."[22]

Zvomuya's work shows that the tussle between Seepe and others is also a tussle about the nature and role of the intellectual. Seepe wrote widely on the topic, arguing that the intellectual's role includes the "search for the truth, the interrogation of the meaning and implications of both public conduct and policy decisions. . . . Least of all should an intellectual be there to make his/her audience feel good: the whole point is to be embarrassing, contrary even unpleasant."[23] The commitment to truth is fundamental to intellectual life, and Seepe appears to argue that it can be achieved only by independence from political groupings and government. For Seepe, to argue in favor of a powerful grouping's interests is by its nature ideological.[24] Shot through much of his critique of the presidency and the ruling party is an assumption that individuals close to power who argue certain positions cannot be true intellectuals, as they avoid confronting critical issues and do not wish to offend the powerful. He calls such people "pseudo-intellectuals," individuals who take on the guise of the intellectual in order to promote embedded political positions. There is more than a little assumption by Seepe of bad faith by the president and those who argue his positions.

Another thorny issue for Seepe was the repeated reference to black (and African) intellectuals and the call on them to engage in public debate in certain prescribed ways. Referring to a call by Mbeki for black intellectuals to be engaged in policy work, he argues that this is an attempt to racialize intellectual work:

How else do we explain the exclusion of white intellectuals? What happened to Mbeki's embracing that everyone is an African? Are there developmental issues and challenges that are no-go areas for white intellectuals? Or are they excluded because they are likely to raise embarrassing questions and expose the intellectual bankruptcy of the ruling class?[25]

Seepe strongly resisted the idea that black thinkers should be homogeneous, confined to particular views and ways of operating.

Seepe's emphasis on independence of thought and speech, independence from government and the powerful, and how this is the only way to truth, draws on the writings of figures he sees as models for public intellectual engagement, particularly Edward Said. In addition, his argument resonates with journalistic professional ideology (as we set it out below), and with notions of the public sphere as a space between the people and the state. Seepe in his writing thus draws from a Western Enlightenment intellectual tradition that gives primacy to the public exercise of reason.

Nobel laureate Archbishop Desmond Tutu entered the discussion in 2004 in the high-profile annual Nelson Mandela Lecture, specifically referring to the practice of labeling critics of government as disloyal or unpatriotic. "I am concerned to see how many have so easily been seemingly cowed and apparently intimidated to comply," he said.[26] President Mbeki responded sharply, treating Tutu's comments as an attempt to silence government and prevent their views from being expressed in public. He asked for "those who present themselves as the greatest defenders of the poor [to] demonstrate decent respect for the truth, rather than indecent resort to empty rhetoric."[27] This exchange was taken up by the media and interpreted by a number of commentators as discrediting Tutu, and seeking to exclude him from public debate.[28]

The ANC's Internet newsletter then produced a three-part article on what it called "The Sociology of the Public Discourse in Democratic South Africa."[29] The core issue, they argued, was a struggle over who sets the national agenda, between "the elite" and the ANC, representing the "overwhelming majority" who voted the party into power. The "elite" were identified as primarily white, but also as including blacks who shared an elite "political and ideological platform." This elite controlled the media and represented elite opinion as "public opinion," a primary tactic by a neoliberal elite in undermining revolutionary gains. Another strategy was using established "icons" whose opinions were positioned as unassailable and whose job was to neutralize opposing voices. In contradistinction to this, public opinion, the article asserted, stems from the "views of the overwhelming majority that supports the ANC." The issue, according to the article, needed to be understood as part of a struggle by Africans to set an African agenda.

The struggle by Africans for an African agenda was the key problematic articulated by the Native Club, a group that announced its arrival in the public arena in 2006 by organizing a conference around this theme. Called "Where Are the Natives? The Black Intelligentsia Today," the conference announcement argued that for Africans to make progress, they would be required to "sever the shackles of intellectual servitude and work towards becoming masters and architects of their own destiny."[30] The advertisement referred to colonialism and racial dehumanization as factors in the alienation of Africans from indigenous culture, which meant "a significant number of African intellectuals find it difficult to think first as Africans, whenever they are confronted by issues that impact directly on the African perspective, mindset and identity." This led to a separation of the intelligentsia from the "majority base, defined and despised as the masses."[31]

The advertisement of the conference was accompanied by an opinion piece by Sandile Memela, identified in the article as a journalist, author, and spokesperson for the Ministry of Arts and Culture. He argued:

> I am troubled by the rise of a hand-picked bunch of black commentators and public intellectuals who opine on freedom of thought, speech and independence and who diss the government at every opportunity. For me, they are coconut intellectuals, white inside. . . . They promote a culture of democracy. . . . But they don't dismantle racist and capitalist assumptions and interests. They don't challenge the status quo.[32]

A heated debate followed in the pages of the print media, and eventually reached Parliament, with opposition party members accusing the presidency of funding a racially exclusive club.[33]

In a study of the media debates, Masango[34] notes that a key issue was the definition of an intellectual. She argues that ideas about intellectuals in South Africa are in line with global ideas (i.e., individuals "deeply involved in books," "cultural experts who use their expertise to speak in public," those in "professional occupations").[35] However, some intellectuals felt the need for "a 'local' definition of who they are." Although race was an important factor in being a "home-grown" intellectual, "being of a black race was no guarantee for one to be a member of the [Native] club and that race by itself was not enough to guarantee 'nativeness,' but a certain kind of loyalty is required."[36] She concludes that intellectuals in South Africa grapple with their position in society in much the same way as other African intellectuals have had to, where a historic positioning of opposition to colonial power becomes compromised by the move of a liberation movement into power.

Masango also asks the question of whether the Native Club operates as a counterpublic. Here she draws on Fraser's[37] critique of the Habermasian imagined public sphere, which proposes a unitary space in which anyone can enter on equal terms and debate issues of the public good. Fraser argues that access to a unitary public sphere in a stratified society is always contingent on a range of factors, and that, in fact, there has always been a multiplicity of publics and public spheres, with various hierarchical relations between them. For deliberation and democratic engagement to allow participation beyond a largely bourgeois elite, some of the subaltern or marginalized groups need to constitute themselves as counterpublics, in which they conduct their own deliberations, before formulating a position from which to intervene in the public sphere.

Masango notes that the Native Club positions itself as if it is a counterpublic in relation to the mainstream media, which they call a "hostile space," but "fails to live up to all the characteristics of a counterpublic in that it does not allow open access and social equality."[38] We would argue further that contained in the notion of the counterpublic is the unequal access to the more powerful spaces in public debate and in society, and the raison d'être for a counterpublic is to contest that power. However, of interest in South Africa is the phenomenon of groupings and individuals close to political power, such as the Native Club, who still position themselves as an oppositional and marginalized counterpublic. In this conception, the media become the place of power they seek to contest.

It is therefore not surprising that the media are not merely a *space* in which debates about intellectuals, the presidency, and public debate are conducted—they are also often the focus for hostilities. Many controversies over the last decade were sparked by developments at South Africa's public broadcaster, the SABC. Previously the dominant force in broadcasting and an institution close to the apartheid state, the SABC had been the focus of a series of transformations since the 1990s. Always in the spotlight, the broadcaster came under increased scrutiny after the appointment of a board in 2004 that hired a former ANC loyalist, Dr. Snuki Zikalala, as news director. The resignations of the CEO, key members of his executive and news teams, and well-respected journalists followed. The canning of a documentary perceived to be critical of President Mbeki; the broadcaster's failure to air the heckling of the deputy president, Phumzile Mlambo-Ngcuka, at a rally; and its perceived positive bias toward Mbeki in its coverage of the presidential succession debate were cited as signs of the broadcaster's waning independence and lack of impartiality.[39]

It was in this context that a report in the *Sowetan* newspaper in 2006 accused the broadcaster of banning certain commentators (mostly black and critical of government policy) from its news and actuality shows. The SABC issued a denial. However, a presenter on the SABC's most respected current affairs program, *AMLive*, in the course of interviewing an executive of the broadcaster revealed that certain commentators were, in fact, blacklisted. This resulted in an uproar, mostly in the pages of the commercial print media, and the SABC instituted a commission of inquiry into the situation. There was further controversy when the board refused to release the inquiry to the media, and the matter is now the subject of a complaint to the broadcasting regulator, the Independent Communications Authority of South Africa (ICASA).[40]

The blacklisting was widely interpreted as a move designed to limit critical commentary about government. There can be little doubt that this was one of the desired effects of the blacklisting and as such it elicited strong responses. But the controversy signaled more than simply a political struggle for control of the public broadcaster. The key underlying struggle, we contend, centered on the definition and understanding of the term "public interest."

In the Public Interest

Close analysis of the controversy[41] reveals two groupings who think in different ways about the public, and about the public's relationship to the state and the media. Interviews with a range of decision makers involved in the controversy demonstrate that certain conceptions of publicness considered fundamental to the professional practice of journalism are vigorously contested. Ideas and definitions of the public, of accountability, and of representivity vary widely. Professional journalists tend to think of the public as continuously engaged with and concerned about issues of the common good, citizenship, and democracy, in other words, a critical and intellectual public that participates continually through media engagement in the day-to-day affairs of the public realm. The *AMLive* journalists involved in the blacklisting dispute thought of themselves as representing this imagined public by virtue of their journalistic practices—interrogating the powerful, allowing a space for diverse voices, and so on.[42]

On the other hand, many executives of the SABC, and members of its board, thought of the public in another way, primarily as the majority of South Africans who voted the government into power, and who are disadvantaged and who have certain developmental needs. In this conception, the government represents the people by virtue of having been elected, and the public broadcaster accounts to the people by accounting to Parliament. This position was largely in agreement with the views of many members of the African National Congress (but not all). It should be noted that the SABC executives also expressed their commitment to public debate, to accountability, and to representing the interests of the people, but held different understandings of what those values meant and how they should be expressed in practice. The key difference was that they understood the people to engage in public deliberation in an episodic manner, by going to the ballot box, thereby providing government with a mandate to determine (and act in) the public interest.

There were also differences in how to conceive of publicness in the operations of public debate in the media. *AMLive* operated in particular ways and with particular values. The news part of the show featured a high percentage of national and serious news that *AMLive* journalists believed to be in the public interest, rather than sensational or entertainment-oriented. The presentation style moved beyond the reporting of events to include substantial comment and analysis. The presenters actively challenged spokespeople, and the team strove to ensure that alternative views and interpretations of events were included in the show's lineup. There was a culture of robust engagement.[43]

The "After Eight Debate," a debate component that followed the news section, often looked specifically for guests who disagreed on an issue, or could argue passionately. Sometimes the presenters themselves played devil's advocate, taking the opposite position in relation to a guest or a caller. However, although the After Eight Debate actively staged argumentative and robust discussion, presenter John Perlman remarked on the tendency for people on the show to seek solutions to problems, thus identifying a strand of potential conciliation within the debate.[44] The presenters coached callers into making cogent points, answering challenges, and following distinct lines of reasoning; and pushed them beyond the expression of opinion, preference, and belief. Likewise, the presenters did substantial work in contextualizing issues, introducing experts, and mediating their inputs in a way that made them accessible to the listeners, facilitating a greater general understanding of the points under discussion.

The *AMLive* case shows that to ensure that public deliberation in the media contributes to democracy and deals with issues of complexity, a high degree of media-based orchestration is needed. This places the onus on journalists, presenters, and producers to be interventionist, skilled at conducting discussions, careful in the choice of commentators, and highly knowledgeable. And this ideally calls a debating, critical, and engaged public into being, a public that acts in a particular mode of democratic citizenship. Thus, a high degree of orchestration is necessary to constitute a debating public on air. This highlights the professional judgments and discretion around inclusion and exclusion exercised by the media professionals involved in putting the program together on a daily basis. Such judgments are made with reference to criteria of expertise, representivity, diversity, and crucially a fuzzy but central notion of acting in the public interest.

While we argue that the orchestrations of the journalists on *AMLive* brought a particular kind of public into being, it is important to note that the journalists did not see themselves as constructing or creating that public. They perceived the program as providing a space for a preexisting public, serving *the* public, which already and automatically operated in an engaged mode of democratic citizenship. The professional ideology of the journalists thus draws on the Enlightenment ideal of debating, rational, critical citizens working toward the common good, and these values are normatively wired into their practice. Thus, they may critically examine the dynamics and limits of their project, but not the fundamental status and value of the project itself. This lack of critical engagement is not confined to the *AM-Live* journalists and producers; debate in the print media about the blacklisting controversy revealed a similar lack of analytic reflection on the founding principles of journalistic professional practice and Enlightenment-derived ideals of democratic citizenship.[45]

Contestation around the concepts of public and public interest indicates that a number of norms that other democracies take for granted remain open for discussion in South Africa. Concepts like the public, with long lineages in Western political thought, are vigorously critiqued, mostly from perspectives originating from an intellectual tradition rooted in national democratic struggle, with Marxist origins and Africanist inflections.

For journalists operating in terms of professional practices rooted in Enlightenment thinking, public connotes the open and shifting space between the market and the state available for operations of critical rationality. In this conceptualization, the role of intellectuals is to fuel deliberation by ensuring that issues are addressed with due attention to their full complexity. It is the intellectuals who bear the burden of drawing the attention of citizens to the long-term implications of their desires, to make the case where appropriate for the good sense of deferring immediate desires, and to spell out any complex ethical implications. In this conceptualization, the independence of the intellectual is highly valorized.

For those SABC executives rooted in a national democratic struggle intellectual tradition, the concept of public operates today with a residual socialist legacy, inflected by nationalism, and an awareness of the experience of colonial and racial relegation of indigenous and class knowledge and values systems. This expresses itself as an adherence to ideas of a social revolution geared toward assertive realization of equality, involving a repositioning of a white elite, and challenging historically white (and allied Western) economic power and values. Here *public* means "the people," whose interests are manifested through the ballot box, who thereby endorse the ANC, and so are assumed to endorse also the national democratic view of equality embedded in its policies. This is the form of public interest being promoted by the SABC executives in deciding to blacklist commentators seen to be critical of the national democratic project. In this conceptualization, the valorized intellectual is the one who thoughtfully advances a national democratic agenda understood as the will of the people.[46] The embeddedness of this intellectual was foreshadowed in the struggle tradition of the ANC as a liberation movement. Indeed, ANC intellectual and academic Raymond Suttner conceptualized the ANC, historically, as "collective intellectual," drawing on diverse forms of knowledge including book learning and grassroots experience.[47]

In identifying the existence of these two different views of publicness, we are able to develop for analytical purposes a theoretical understanding of public—a meta-concept of publicness—that is distinct from either of these everyday understandings of publicness. Our investigation reveals that in both of these everyday conceptions, the public is understood as a preconstituted entity—it exists outside of the protagonists, like the population of a country. However, Fraser has argued that there are multiple publics, deliberating and contesting in relation to each other, and in ways not envisaged by Habermas. Michael Warner goes further in arguing that not only is there no one preexisting public, but that publics exist only by the virtue of their imagining, and they come into being in relation to particular texts and the circulation of those texts.[48]

In the media, publics come into being in relation to different kinds of production, in this case, the production of *AMLive* and the After Eight Debate. So, in fact, the kind of public deliberation that took place, or perhaps the kind of debating public engaged by *AMLive* in 2006, was brought together by the particular operations and practices of the producers and presenters of the program. That public could exist and debate in the way it did only because the operations of the program had the effect of "orchestrating" that kind of debate. Drawing from this, we propose a third conception of public—distinguished from the other not by being differently constituted but by being more of a *meta*, or analytical, concept. It is neither a preexisting, engaged but elite public in the Habermasian mode, nor an inert mass that has mandated the ruling party to act for it, but an "orchestrated public," which comes into being through the practices and operations of media professionals in the production of debate. This public can be recognized at the level of analysis, but cannot be operationalized until a form of orchestration, based on an imagined public, occurs.

What are the implications for intellectuals, then, in the orchestrations of media? As we have shown, producing public debate in the media requires media gatekeepers to make a range of choices. They make decisions about whom to include in debate, and what is in the public interest to debate, according to norms of practice rooted in Enlightenment concepts. In the course of these processes, they valorize certain commentators, such as Sipho Seepe. Leaders of public institutions and government-based intellectuals steeped in the legacy of national democratic struggle define public interest differently and valorize different commentators, using different criteria. However, the lines between these two positions are far from absolute. Certain journalists and certain leaders of public institutions or government intellectuals operate in ways cognizant of and sympathetic to elements of arguments from "the other side."

In addition, two threads typically crisscross both positions. The first is recognition of the necessity of negotiating the legacies of racism. As commentator Xolela Mangcu argues, race is a key and problematic concept for South African society, one that needs to be constantly critiqued and unsettled.[49] Although it should be recognized that race is a social construct, it has been in South Africa a construct that defined and structured life and experience in oppressive and deeply invasive ways, and continues to do so. Although "playing the race card" is sometimes seen as a strategy to duck critique, both views of public interest recognize the need to attend to questions of race. The second strand of deliberation concerns the ongoing aura of suspicion that surrounds the Enlightenment inheritance as a consequence of the role that its forms of knowledge production played historically in underwriting colonial and apartheid oppression, suspicions not confined to those steeped in national democratic struggle thinking.

Where currently many intellectuals speak passionately from one or the other of the two main positions delineated above, our chapter suggests that the challenge is to negotiate this complex terrain in a manner alive to its fullest complexity. It is only through a critically and analytical understanding of the philosophical legacies these positions draw on that can we craft routes forward for forms of South African modernity and active citizenship that are ethical, illuminate contemporary and historical conditions, and are capable of carrying us productively into the future. We also need to engage with some of the limitations at the heart of these conceptions. For example, Enlightenment ideas of public sphere and rational critical debate do privilege elites. This is a problem for all societies, but especially societies where the elite were installed as a result of the violent dispossession of colonialism (and, in South Africa, maintained through a repressive system of racial hierarchy). On the other hand, the majoritarian (and developmental) position acts in the interests of the dispossessed majority in a top-down arrangement that is unregulated except intermittently by the ballot box, and open to abuse. The challenge, then, for intellectuals in South Africa and other African states, is to find an analytical position able to illuminate these contradictions and deal with them. If we do not, the contestation becomes a fight between elites in which the majority do not have a voice. Public deliberation is then reduced to an instrument by which a small elite debates issues and decision making for the entire society.

Notes

This chapter is one of a series of interlocked papers produced by the Constitution of Public Intellectual Life Research Project, University of the Witwatersrand. Our thanks are due to the core group of the project for their ongoing engagement with this work. It was first presented at the "African Intellectuals and Decolonization" Conference, Ohio University, October 2008.

1. Slavko Splichal, "In Search of a Strong European Public Sphere: Some Critical Observations on Conceptualizations of Publicness and the (European) Public Sphere," *Media, Culture, and Society* 28, no. 5 (2006): 699.

2. Jurgen Habermas, *The Structural Transformation of the Public Sphere: An Inquiry into a Category of Bourgeois Society*, trans. Thomas Burger and Frederick Lawrence (Cambridge, MA: MIT Press, 1989).

3. Antonio Gramsci, *Selections from the Prison Notebooks* (London: Lawrence and Wishart, 1971), 9.

4. Edward W. Said, *Representations of the Intellectual* (London: Vintage, 1994), 71.

5. Pamela J. Shoemaker, *Gatekeeping* (London: Sage, 1991).

6. This chapter draws on the work, discussions, and collective thinking of the Wits University journalism program's Media and Public Debate research cluster of 2004 to 2007, led by Lesley Cowling and Carolyn Hamilton, and comprising honors students Nazeem Dramat, Refiloe Lepere, Rehana Roussouw, Shirona Patel, and Percy Zvomuya; and master's students Rebecca Kahn, Philile Masango, and Kenichi Serino.

7. Carolyn Hamilton, "Uncertain Citizenship and Public Deliberation in Post-Apartheid South Africa," *Social Dynamics* 35, no. 2 (2009): 355–74.

8. Ibid.

9. See Jacques Louw, "Journalism and the Law," in *Changing the Fourth Estate: Essays on South African Journalism*, ed. Adrian Hadland (Cape Town: HSRC Press, 2005), 121–30.

10. Based on a discussion in October 2007 with Franz Kruger, who headed SABC radio news from 1995 to 2000.

11. Lesley Cowling, "South Africa," in *Global Entertainment Media: Content, Audiences, Issues*, ed. Anne Cooper-Chen (Mahwah, NJ: Lawrence Erlbaum, 2005), 121–25.

12. See, for example, the contributions of, among others, Vusi Gumede, Alan Hirsch, and Bheki Khumalo, and Mbeki's speeches, collected on the Mbeki Page, http://www.anc.org.za/ancdocs/history/mbeki/.

13. "Nepad in Brief, 2005," The New Partnership for Africa's Development: Nepad, http://www.nepad.org/2005/files/inbrief.php.

14. See Ivor Chipkin, "Democracy and Dictatorship," *Social Dynamics* 35, no. 2 (2009): 375–93. Mbeki's "authoritarianism" was a concern within the African National Congress, trade union movement, and South African Communist Party. Various commentators in the media also criticized him personally, for example, Sipho Seepe (see discussion in this chapter), Justice Malala, and Xolela Mangcu.

15. Hamilton, "Uncertain Citizenship."

16. Chipkin, "Democracy and Dictatorship."

17. Percy Zvomuya, "Sipho Seepe: The Making of a Public Intellectual" (honors thesis, Wits University, 2005).

18. Sipho Seepe, *Speaking Truth to Power* (Pretoria: Vista University and Skotaville Media, 2004), 216.

19. Ibid., 224.

20. Zvomuya, "Sipho Seepe."

21. Seepe, *Speaking Truth to Power*, 26.

22. Zvomuya, "Sipho Seepe," 21.

23. Seepe, *Speaking Truth to Power*, 69.

24. Zvomuya, "Sipho Seepe," 19.

25. Seepe, *Speaking Truth to Power*, 67.

26. Desmond Tutu, "Look to the Rock from Which You Were Hewn," in *The Lectures: The Nelson Mandela Annual Lecture* (Johannesburg: Nelson Mandela Foundation, 2006), 32.

27. "Letter from the President," *ANC Today* 4, no. 47 (November 26, 2004), http://www.anc.org.za/docs/anctoday/2004/at47.htm.

28. Justice Malala, "A Sense of Siege," *Financial Mail*, February 4, 2005.

29. "The Sociology of the Public Discourse in Democratic South Africa," *ANC Today*, January 14, 21, and 28, 2005, http://www.anc.org.za/list.php?t=ANC%20Today&y=2005

30. "Where Are the Natives? The Black Intelligentsia Today," *Mail and Guardian*, May 5–11, 2006, 19.

31. Ibid.

32. Sandile Memela, "Black Brainpower," *Mail and Guardian*, May 5–11, 2006, 19.

33. Wyndham Hartley, "Native Club 'Not President's Project,'" *Business Day*, July 10, 2006.

34. Philile Masango, "An Analysis of the Engagements of Intellectuals and Intellectual Activity in the South African Media: A Case Study of the Native Club" (master's thesis, University of the Witwatersrand, 2009).

35. Ibid., 47.

36. Ibid., 48.

37. Nancy Fraser, "Rethinking the Public Sphere: A Contribution to the Critique of Actually Existing Democracy," in *Habermas and the Public Sphere*, ed. Craig Calhoun (Cambridge, MA: MIT Press, 1992), 109–42.

38. Masango, "An Analysis," 51.

39. Rhoda Kadalie, "Secrets and Lies: Time for Zikalala to Take the Stand," *Business Day*, June 29, 2006.

40. Nazeem Dramat, "The SABC and the 'Blacklist' Controversy: Professionalism and Resistance," *Rhodes Journalism Review* 27 (2007): 62.

41. We draw here on our more detailed analysis of the blacklisting saga in Lesley Cowling and Carolyn Hamilton, "Thinking Aloud/Allowed: Pursuing the Public Interest in Radio Debate" (paper presented at "Paradoxes of the Postcolonial Public Sphere: South African Democracy at the Crossroads," conference at Wits University, January 2008).

42. Rehana Rossouw, "The SABC and the 'Blacklist' Controversy: Understanding 'Accountability,'" *Rhodes Journalism Review* 27 (2007): 64.

43. Lesley Cowling and Carolyn Hamilton, "Thinking Aloud/Allowed: Pursuing the Public Interest in Radio Debate," *Social Dynamics*, 36, no. 1 (2010): 85–98.

44. Ibid.

45. Shirona Patel, "The SABC and the 'Blacklist' Controversy: Policing the Aberration," *Rhodes Journalism Review* 27 (2007): 65.

46. Our analysis here draws on Peter Hudson, "Taking the Democratic Subject Seriously" (paper presented to the Symposium on Cosmopolitan Citizenship, Human Sciences Research Council, April 2007); as well as on Ivor Chipkin, *Do South Africans Exist?: Nationalism, Democracy and the Identity of "the People"* (Johannesburg: Wits University Press, 2007).

47. Raymond Suttner, "The Character and Formation of Intellectuals within the ANC-Led South African Liberation Movement," in *African Intellectuals: Rethinking Politics, Language, Gender and Development*, ed.

Thandika Mkandawire (Dakar and London: CODESRIA and Zed Books, 2005), 117–54.

48. Michael Warner, *Publics and Counterpublics* (New York: Zone Books, 2002).

49. Xolela Mangcu, "Evidentiary Genocide: Intersections of Race, Power and the Archive," in *Becoming Worthy Ancestors*, ed. Xolela Mangcu (Johannesburg: Wits University Press, 2009).

Setting the Agenda for Decolonizing African Media Systems

Ebenezer Adebisi Olawuyi

Introduction

The role of the media in the sociopolitical transformation of any society is never in doubt; in fact, the media have been described as a catalyst for speeding up developmental processes. The media's capacity to disseminate information, express divergent voices and views, and help form public opinion on issues as well as facilitate debate has been a high-water mark in the pursuit of their social mandate. These classical roles, which have characteristically defined the functional role of the media across different geographical divides, "gave legitimacy to the activities of the media and to their existence as the Fourth Estate."[1]

The media as the Fourth Estate serves as the guardian of the people vis-à-vis the three branches of government, namely, the executive, the legislative, and the judiciary. Constitutionally, these three branches make for "good government" as they "check and balance" one another. However, in a democracy, government cannot be trusted blindly, since government can be stronger than the governed. Consequently, there is the need for a "checker and balancer," and that is how the media through history have come to be regarded as the tribune of the people.[2]

However, Lohmus is of the opinion that there are internal contradictions between the "normative" naming of the processes and the actual relevant content of the media, when their role is considered in society.[3] The media are active participants in the social processes, but the profile of engagement can be more endogenous or exogenous, more active or passive, more critical or noncritical.[4]

Aside from the media serving as vehicles for transmitting knowledge, they have also, in the course of discharging this oversight function brought to bear alongside their reportage, a subtle yet profound interpretation that has redefined people's value perception of the "actual" world. McCombs and Reynolds noted that "not only do the news media largely determine our awareness of the world at large, supplying the major elements for our pictures of the world, they also influence the prominence of these elements in the picture."[5] Invariably, the "mass media have come largely to determine the cognitive and affective perceptions of the non-local world through their portrayal of events, issues, people and places."[6]

Further still, the sense of unity among people that has been created and sustained by such powerful identities as defined by religion, nationality, and work has been grossly undermined by the powerful representation of the media in the process of shaping social life. Thus, the media's ability to construct people's social identities, in terms of both a sense of unity and a sense of difference, may be their most powerful and important effect.[7] As such, the construction of reality by the media has come to be accepted as the valid representation of the actual world. It is therefore apparent that beyond its "natural" domain, the media wield impregnable influence in the construction of aspects of "reality" such as people, places, objects, events, cultural identities, and other abstract concepts.[8]

Ignored in virtually every discussion of Africa is the effect of colonialism on the continent. Eighty years of colonialism by the European powers left an indelible stain on Africa that is difficult to erase.[9] Reiterating this position, the former president of Zambia, Kenneth Kaunda, argued that colonialism devalued Africans, for "it created elite societies in which men's worth was determined by an irrelevant biological detail—skin pigmentation." It also "dinned into the African mind the idea that we are primitive, backward, and degraded, and but for their (European) presence amongst us, we would be living like animals."[10] It is that colonial legacy that still colors the reporting—or the lack of it—on Africa and makes it difficult to present accurate images of the continent and its peoples to the Western world.

Since journalistic traditions in Africa are historically inherited from the West, it is expected that some parallels in terms of form and content in practice should be evident. As a matter of fact, the development of the mass media in Africa can be traced to colonialism. The establishment of African media systems by colonial governments was perceived to be "a benevolent gesture of tutelage to the colonial people."[11] This means that the establishment of the media in Africa was primarily to serve colonial interest and not to cater to the advancement of Africa or Africans. Therefore, the media became a conduit for indoctrinating Africans. For example, films were introduced into Africa, among other reasons, "to help the adult African to understand and adapt himself to the new conditions (the British way of life) which are invading and threatening to overwhelm him."[12]

Luke Uche further argues that colonial influence on Africa has been quite domineering even in the postindependence era.[13] According to him, this influence

> is particularly noticeable in the area of the mass media contents. Due to lack of skilled manpower as well as essential infrastructure to sustain the independence of the emergent nation-states, the former colonial overlords consciously used technical aid schemes (especially in the areas of training in newspaper, radio and television) as strategies for ensuring the preservation of, and continued dependence on their cherished values and ideological inclinations in their former colonies.

In spite of more than five decades of media operations in the postcolonial era, African media have still not been able to evolve an articulate and robust media system that is independent of the West. The reason for this can be attributed to inadequate financial, technical, and telecommunication resources; lack of professional manpower; and a legacy of slavery, apartheid, colonialism, and imperialism.[14] Consequently, the media in Africa manifest the following characteristic traits:

1. Skewed, urban-based centralization of infrastructure, resources and audiences;
2. Emphasis on comings and goings and images of top national political leaders, particularly the president;
3. Heavy and often conflicting demands on media institutions to serve national development, to inform, educate and entertain;
4. General lack of diversity of information and focus between different national media organs;
5. Structure that ensures top-down communications flow and is susceptible to monopolization and political manipulation.[15]

As a result of the issues enumerated above, the "continent continues to depend on external media imports for information and entertainment, the cultures of its various nations are continually being eclipsed by external cultural influences due to a wholesale dependence on foreign media products."[16] Against this background, this is a call to action for African media intellectuals to decolonize its media system from the continued influence of Western imperialists and their transnational media conglomerates who have continually dictated the pace and tempo of media contents and practice in the world.

Western Media and African Reality

Studies have established that the media in the coverage and selection of news are "far from conveying 'value-free' or 'ideology-free' objective reality." Rather, they "actively help to construct and reconstruct social reality by presenting a particular news frame."[17] The method employed by the media in the selection and interpretation of events, what they focus on and what they omit, helps to define public knowledge as well as the construction of public opinion.[18] The increasing Western influence on the journalistic style and performances of African media has redefined the entire spectrum of mass media operation in the continent. Therefore, Western ideologies characterize the construction of media narratives.

The collapse of space, that is, a country's borderline that comes with the process of globalization, has further taken its toll on the nature and character of the media in Africa. The effects, unfortunately, have been a widening gulf between developed countries of the North and their developing counterparts in the Northern Hemisphere, and most worrisome is the imbalance that it perpetuates among nations, especially between countries of the industrialized North and developing South.[19] Obviously, journalistic practices, strategies of representation, and definitions of the situation, among other factors, have been influenced as a result of the political and economic considerations that inevitably make it almost impossible for the media to fulfill its watchdog function.[20] Therefore, the media as an "institution is both affected by globalization and is itself an agent of it."[21] Accordingly, the content and structure of international news, as well as its influence on the sociopolitical processes that depend on this system of public communication, have been altered significantly.[22] Therefore, the media are no longer a part of a distinct political geography; rather, they play a crucial role in creating and rearticulating boundaries of spaces in which social communications are constructed.

Emmanuel Egwu argues that as a result of Western countries' superior advantage in the ownership and control of systems of communication, they have unfairly employed the mass media to create, most especially in the South of Africa, a society of mass passivity, mass response, and retroactivity, the effect of which has produced an acquiescent society whose attitudes, values, beliefs, motives, aspirations, living, tastes, and styles have almost become molded along Western sensibilities.[23]

Also, the Western dominance of the global mediascape has not only perpetuated imbalance in the information exchange between the West and African countries, but, unfortunately, promoted images of Africa typified by "vicious harmful insults, based on biases and stereotypes and prejudices."[24] In the same vein, McNelly pointed out that it is not just a question of being projected abroad in what is considered a distorted manner, but a question of African people being projected to themselves in the same distorted manner by Western-dominated media.[25]

The fact cannot be denied that the image of Africa as represented in the Western media is conscientiously "focused on sensational, mostly negative, events that are often colored with nineteenth century and colonial European bias."[26] The type of news that gets reported about the continent is influenced in the main by the general values and organizational demands of the Western media. News, therefore, is not merely the random reporting of events, but rather is constructed and shaped by journalists who determine what is newsworthy or not and the treatment or slant of the report. Lack of interest in covering Africa, coupled with inadequate resources dedicated to engaging reporters who are well familiar with the continent's sociocultural antecedents, is also responsible for the malicious treatment Africa receives in Western media. As a result of this, Western media typically oversimplify complex events and settings, thereby creating stereotypes that become fixed in the minds of news consumers.[27]

This chauvinistic editorial policy of Western media is evidently influenced and sustained by their normative culture; which has resulted in contradictions and identity crisis for the continent of Africa. When one considers how "Africa has been used as a topos, a theme, a trope, how in short, it has been metaphorized"[28] by Western media, one may not be too surprised. After all, they believe "it is all told in the Bible."[29] In other words, it's divine that Africa perpetually occupies the base of the ladder. This perhaps explains the reason behind the nineteenth-century European colonization of Africa; as they "gave themselves the self-appointed duty or burden of helping their unfortunate African brethren by colonizing them in order to put them back on the road to 'progress' and 'civilization.'"[30] To this end, Western bias may be understandable.

It is important to note that Africans themselves have not adopted a *sidon look* posture at the gross indiscretion of the West through its media. Africa's heads of government, scholars, and media practitioners, as well as concerned citizens, "have been deeply worried that negative stories and apocalyptic pictures" dominate the Western media and scare away visitors,[31] and potential investors, thereby leaving the continent in a state of developmental flux.

Several measures have been adopted to mitigate the persistent negative image of Africa in the Western media. The high point is the establishment of the International Commission for the Study of Communication Problems, also known as the MacBride Commission, by UNESCO's General Conference that was held between October and November 1976 in Nairobi, Kenya. The commission was saddled with the responsibility of studying the question of how to maintain national and cultural sovereignty in the face of globalization of the mass media, while emphasizing the crucial role of communication in sustaining international understanding.[32]

These efforts brought to the fore the urgent need to address the lingering news flow crisis between developed and developing countries. The truth of the matter is that the commission lacked the political resolve to achieve much, as it also had to contend with the stiff opposition from the United States and Britain, who perceived the entire exercise as a deliberate attempt to censor press freedom. The United States particularly viewed the demand for the New World Information and Communication Order (NWICO) as an attempt by leaders of developing countries to subordinate media activities to the whims and caprices of those in government. This it considered a violation of the very principle of the First Amendment. On the contrary, Britain's resistance is predicated on the inviolability of press freedom. Consequently, Africa has had to contend with the painful reality of being branded negatively in the Western media.[33]

Unfortunately, Western journalists have severally defended their journalistic style and performance. They "claim that international news coverage, like its domestic equivalent, is objective, truthful, and unbiased, and that what they report is 'the way it really is.'" Furthermore, they said, "if certain developing countries want better press, they should hire Madison Avenue public relations firms to improve their images abroad."[34]

Western media's continuous denial of misrepresenting reality in Africa clearly indicates their unrepentant commitment to a "business as usual" editorial style as well as the near impossibility of achieving a cease-fire in the news flow crisis in north-south relations. Therefore, Africa has a moral responsibility to herself "to offset the negative effects of inaccurate or malicious reporting" of the Western press by putting in place tangible structures that would facilitate "the full and factual presentation of news"[35] about her to the rest of the world.

Versi is of the opinion that Africans cannot continue to rely on Western media to undo the "harm" done to the continent through their media outlets. Rather, "we must fight to present Africa in its true, glorious colors."[36] According to him, this can be achieved only through counteracting negativity and replacing it "with a positive, shining image of our great continent."

It is worth stating that the views expressed hitherto do not suggest that African media should engage in the ignoble business of laundering the image of the continent. What is pertinent is that "missing from these lurid news reports are the central issues of human beings of all colors and their attempts to build stable societies around them."[37] This is the honest image of Africa that is lacking in the Western media narratives on the continent. Therefore, African media have a moral burden to fill this missing link in their own coverage of the continent.

Toward a Normative Theory of African Media Operations

The underlying aim of media researchers and theorists "is to formulate statements or propositions that will have some explanatory power"[38] on how the communications media facilitate social change, as well as "to solve empirical, conceptual, and practical problems"[39] that media studies have provoked. Media theory, therefore, is aimed at improving the understanding of the mass communication process by providing platforms to make predictions, and possibly control the consequences of the mass communication process, as observed in the social world.[40]

Miller observed that the development of theory is not an enterprise carried out in isolation from others.[41] Rather, it is derived from a philosophy that is strongly influenced by the domain of what is believed to count as theory and its functional application. This perhaps validates the plethora of media theories, oftentimes overlapping, which have provided significant insights into the understanding of mass media processes and operations.

In explaining the expected role of the African media as champions of African ideals, the normative theory has been identified to provide the framework to justify the propositions that this chapter advocates. Normative theory "describes an ideal way for a media system to be structured and operated."[42] It refers to the "ideas of right and responsibility that underlie . . . expectations of benefit from the media to individuals and society."[43] This theory also provides a significant signpost in understanding the relationship between the media and society. Siebert, Peterson, and Schramm provided a more incisive description of the normative theory in their book *Four Theories of the Press*. According to them, the "press always takes on the form and coloration of the social and political structures within which it operates."[44] What is clear from the normative theory, especially as explained by Baran and Davis and McQuail,[45] is that this theory seeks to prescribe the benchmark for media behavior "in the wider public interest," which is influenced in the main by the following sources: social and political theory; professional theory and practice; the public as citizens (public opinion); the public as audience; the media market; the state and its agencies; and interested parties in the society.[46]

Since what is chiefly expected of responsible media anywhere in the world is the provision of "a full, truthful, comprehensive and intelligent account of the day's events in a context which gives them meaning,"[47] how this is accomplished should be determined by the needs assessment of the individual society, and not a borrowed mechanism that does not take into consideration the peculiarities of a sociopolitical clime. This has been the undoing of the African media whose journalistic style and performances are caricatures of Western media, so that they have not been able to set the agenda for the decolonization of the continent.

African Media Intellectuals and the Agenda to Decolonize African Media

The normative theory of the media holds that for the media to deliver on its social mandate, there is an ideal way for it to be structured and operated. Again, it is important to restate that this theory does not "describe things as they are, nor do they provide scientific explanations or predictions. Instead, they describe the way things *should be* if some ideal values or principles are to be realized."[48] It is in line with this thought that this chapter attempts to *describe*, at the risk of sounding *prescriptive*, what the role of African media intellectuals should be in the arduous task of decolonizing one of the most important social institutions in the continent, the media.

The overwhelming influence of the journalistic style and performance of the West in shaping the contents and programs of African media is a violation of the philosophical base of African ethos. "It retards the evolution of local ideological direction" because "the elements of the news ideology emphasize the extent to which the news is a construction of social reality."[49] Therefore, media messages and contents in Africa should "reflect a construction of a social reality within the ideological context" of the continent.[50] If the media's role is to provide "a window on the world" or write "the first draft of history," then it is expedient to find out whether African media have discharged this function without resorting to the use of the prejudices, values, fears, and distortions of the Western editors.[51] In this way, an issue that urgently begs for the attention of African intellectuals as part of the critical issues that they have to tackle in decolonizing the media in Africa is to radically overhaul media studies curriculum in the continent. This new curriculum should take into cognizance the peculiar nature of the sociopolitical dynamics of the African culture, while its philosophical undercurrent should be defined by African ideals. This does not, however, suggest that Western journalistic ideals should be discarded wholesale; my argument is that, where such ideals would be needed, they should be domesticated to reflect the African experience.

Using the Nigerian experience as an example, a media scholar, Professor Umar Pate of the University of Maiduguri, Nigeria, noted that the bane of journalism training in Nigeria is that the curriculum is based on Western conceptual and theoretical underpinnings.[52] Potential journalists are therefore trained using foreign models that they find absolutely difficult to contextualize within African social reality. He suggests that in strengthening our training capacities, there is the need to fully expose our students to the history, systems, dynamics, geography, successes, and challenges of the Nigerian nation. Besides, they need to be equipped with the right skills as well as sensitized to appreciate their unique roles as professional journalists within the context of a developing country in a globalizing world.

Regrettably, Africa lacks a social philosophy for its communication system.[53] The reason for this is the failure of our media scholars to develop authentic theories as well as a research tradition to deal with the myriad of social communication challenges confronting the continent.[54] The onus, therefore, is on African intellectuals to develop an authentic and articulate African philosophy of communication that is capable of explaining how Africans use their indigenous communication systems to make sense of their existence and interpret their worldview. The efforts of African scholars such as Andrew Moemeka, Charles Okigbo, Kwasi Ansu-Kyeremeh, and Isaac Obeng-Quaidoo, to mention a few, are quite commendable because they point out the values that are inherent in developing our indigenous communication systems. Emerging scholars in African Studies as well as media and communication studies should also build on the foundations that these works have established by providing sound theoretical frameworks as well as research traditions that would describe the normative culture of African indigenous media systems.

Because the media in Africa are a product of colonialism, journalistic style and performances are conceivably determined by the systems and processes of the media in the West. It is not surprising that the treatment of news in African media is patterned after that of the West. Invariably, news of disasters, crimes, accidents, and all manner of negativity dominate news headlines. Realizing the need to rethink media curriculum in developing countries, including Africa, in 2005 UNESCO convened a meeting of journalism educators to develop a journalism curriculum "that would be suitable for use in Developing countries and emerging democracies."[55] The thrust of the curriculum is to teach would-be-practitioners "how to cover political and social issues of particular importance to their *own* society through courses developed in co-operation with other departments in the college or university."[56]

Even the UN recognizes the role of African media intellectuals in creating a new media curriculum that would "prepare students to be

critical of their own and others' journalism practice."[57] While rework-
ing the media curriculum to suit our peculiar normative clime, it is
also instructive that African media intellectuals should at the same
time attempt to redefine certain concepts, especially in journalism
practice, that have worked to our disadvantage. For instance, there
is the urgent task of operationalizing concepts such as "news" and
"news value." It is important to note that at the heart of the international news flow crisis is what constitutes news. This apparently
sets the tone for the seemingly intractable problems that have characterized North-South information dialogue. However, what has made
the situation more problematic to resolve is the ideological undercurrent in the various arguments and counterarguments on these issues.
The pertinence of the issue at hand is that machineries should be put
in place to ensure that news treatment reflects news as both a national
resource and an educational tool. Emphasis, therefore, should be on
the objective presentation of issues and events with the aim of creating awareness and stimulating interest based on didactic values, even
when these are not overtly stated.[58]

Conclusion

This chapter has provided a description of the African mediascape to
argue that African media intellectuals have the onerous task of setting into motion the decolonization process of the media on the continent. Africa is in a state of social, economic, and political flux, and
as a result of the crises that engulf some sections of the continent,
humanitarian conditions are worsening. However, amid the cloud of
hopelessness that seems to hang over the continent, there are significant efforts taking place within Africa to reverse the ugly trends that
would birth the *new* Africa.

According to Rasheed, the "current dominant trend in Africa is,
however, one of unremitting economic and human crises and growing marginalization."[59] He reiterated that in the twenty-first century,
"Africa has no choice but to reverse these unacceptable trends. The
potential, in terms of the natural and human resources, is there; the
positive forces as manifested in the surge towards democratization
and popular participation in development, are already at work. This
translates into the conviction that, bleak and disturbing as the current trends and their implications are, the possibility of turning these

bitter realities into an opportunity does exist."[60] As a matter of fact, the words of Rasheed indicate the preparedness of African leaders to turn around the fortunes of the continent. In order to achieve what appears to be *mission impossible*, as well as to see to the sustenance of the structures that are being put in place, African media need to reappraise their role as critical components in the development of the continent. African media can play this role effectively only when their current systems and processes are redefined to reflect the normative requirements of the continent.

In achieving this, it is pertinent that the task of ensuring that the media live up to this normative responsibility be not entirely left in their hands. Rather, achievement requires different segments of the society, most significantly African media intellectuals, to work in harmony with other stakeholders. Their terms of reference in the main will be to put in place an enduring structure that would lead to the evolution of national communication systems in the continent. This framework should, among other things, articulate policy objectives to drive decisions that would reflect national orientations and an ideological base that is deeply rooted in African philosophy.

The position of this chapter is that African media intellectuals have to set the agenda through discourses and disputations on the imperative of decolonizing African media from the stranglehold of Western media hegemony. This can be achieved through the following: rethinking the conceptual orientation of media curriculum to reflect the peculiar philosophical thought of Africa; seriously and urgently considering the development of indigenous African media systems; and rethinking African media content to address the continent's development challenge. It is only on this platform that African media can be relevant to the social, economic, and political reconstruction of the continent.

Notes

1. Jan Ekecrantz, "Public Spaces, Historical Times and Media Modernities: Media and Historical Spaces," in *Contesting the Frontiers: Media and Dimensions of Identity*, ed. Ullamaija Kivikuru (Goteborg: Nordicom, 2001), 21.

2. Adrian E. Cristobal, "State of the Fourth Estate: 'There Were Three Estates in Parliament but in the Reporter's Gallery Yonder, There Sat a

Fourth Estate More Important Than They All.' —Edmund Burke," *Manila Bulletin* (April 12, 2007), http://www.questia.com.

3. Maarja Lohmus, "Staging Journalism: Professional Identity and Roles of Journalists in Social Changes," in Kivikuru, *Contesting the Frontiers*, 187–207.

4. Kaarle Nordenstreng and Peeter Vihalemm, quoted in Lohmus, "Staging Journalism."

5. Maxwell McCombs and Amy Reynolds, "News Influence on Our Pictures of the World," in *Media Effects: Advances in Theory and Research*, ed. Jennings Bryant and Dolf Zillmann (Mahwah, NJ: Lawrence Erlbaum, 1994), 4.

6. Wale Adebanwi, "The Press and the Politics of Marginal Voices: Narratives of the Experiences of the Ogoni of Nigeria," in *Media, Culture, and Society* 26, no. 6 (2004): 763.

7. Lawrence Grossberg, Ellen Wartella, D. Charles Whitney, and J. Macgregor Wise, *Media Making: Mass Media in a Popular Culture* (Thousand Oaks, CA: Sage, 1998).

8. David Chandler, "Notes on Representation," November 1998, http://www.aber.ac.uk/media/Modules/MC30820/represent.html.

9. Ronald H. Pahl, "The Image of Africa in Our Classrooms," *Social Studies* 86, no. 6 (1995): 246, http://www.questia.com.

10. Kenneth Kaunda, quoted in Pahl, "The Image of Africa."

11. Jengo, quoted in Onyero Mgbejume, *Film in Nigeria: Developments, Problems and Promise*, African Media Monograph Series 7 (Kenya: African Council on Communication Education, 1989).

12. L. A. Notcutt and G. C. Latham, quoted in Mgbejume, *Film in Nigeria*.

13. Luke U. Uche, "Ideology, Theory and Professionalism in the African Mass Media," *African Media Review* 5, no. 1 (1991): 3.

14. W. A. Hachten and A. De Beer, quoted in Emmanuel C. Alozie, "What Did They Say? African Media Coverage of the First 100 Days of the Rwanda Crisis," in *The Media and the Rwanda Genocide*, ed. Allan Thompson (Kampala: Fountain Publishers, 2007), 211–30.

15. J. J. Zaffiro, quoted in Alozie, "What Did They Say?" 212.

16. Uche, "Ideology, Theory and Professionalism," 3.

17. Young C. Yoon and E Gwangho, "Framing International Conflicts in Asia: A Comparative Analysis of News Coverage of Tokdo," in *Media and Conflict: Framing Issues, Making Policy, Shaping Opinions*, ed. Eytan Gilboa (Adsley, NY: Transnational, 2002), 89–116.

18. Annabelle Sreberny-Mohammadi, "Global News Media Cover the World," in *Questioning the Media: A Critical Introduction*, ed. John Downing, Ali Mohammadi, and Annabelle Sreberny-Mohammadi, 2nd ed. (Thousands Oaks, CA: Sage, 1995), 428–43.

19. Manuel Castells, quoted in W. Edward Steinmueller, "ICTs and the Possibilities for Leapfrogging by Developing Countries," *International Labour Review* 140, no. 2 (2001): 193–210.

20. Ekecrantz, "Public Spaces."

21. Stig Hjarvard, quoted in Ekecrantz, "Public Spaces," 15–33.

22. Ibid.

23. Emmanuel U. Egwu, "Foreign Media Projection of Africa: The Role of African Communicators," *Nigerian Journal of Communication* 1, no. 1 (2001): 1–13.

24. Festus Eribo, "Global News Flow in Africa: Nigerian Media Coverage of International News, 1979–1995," *Western Journal of Black Studies* 23, no. 3 (1999): 154, http://www.questia.com.

25. J. T. McNelly, quoted in Eribo, "Global News Flow in Africa," 154.

26. Pahl, "The Image of Africa."

27. Tsan-Kuo Chang and Jae-Won Lee, "Factors Affecting Gatekeeper's Selection of Foreign News: A National Survey of Newspaper Editors," *Journalism Quarterly* 69, no. 3 (1992): 554–61; Mellisa Wall, "An Analysis of News Magazine Coverage of the Rwanda Crisis in the United States," in Thompson, *The Media and the Rwanda Genocide*, 261–76.

28. Ayo Kehinde, "Writing the Fatherland: The Image of Africa in Selected Fictions of Africans in Europe" (paper presented at the "International Workshop on African Presence in Europe," Antwerp, Belgium, November 14–18, 2005), 6.

29. Walter Rodney, *How Europe Underdeveloped Africa* (Abuja: Panaf, 1972), 25.

30. Buluda A. Itandala, "European Images of Africa from Early Times to the Eighteenth Century," in *Images of Africa: Stereotypes and Realities*, ed. Daniel M. Megara (Trenton, NJ: Africa World Press, 2001), 61–81.

31. Anver Versi, "A Positive Image for Africa," *African Business*, no. 5 (May 2001), http://www.questia.com.

32. Sean MacBride, *Many Voices, One World* (Ibadan: Ibadan University Press, 1980).

33. Versi, "A Positive Image for Africa."

34. Sreberny-Mohammadi, "Global News Media."

35. MacBride, *Many Voices.*

36. Versi, "A Positive Image for Africa," 5.

37. Pahl, "The Image of Africa."

38. Werner J. Severin and James W. Tankard Jr., *Communication Theories: Origins, Methods, and Uses in the Mass Media* (New York: Hastings House, 2001), 11.

39. Katherine Miller, *Communication Theories: Perspectives, Processes, and Contexts.* (Boston: McGrawHill, 2002), 22.

40. Severin and Tankard, *Communication Theories.*

41. Miller, *Communication Theories.*

42. Stanley J. Baran and Dennis K. Davis, *Mass Communication Theory: Foundations, Ferment, and Future* (Belmont, CA: Wadsworth/Thomas, 2003), 93.

43. Denis McQuail, *McQuail's Mass Communication Theory*, 5th ed. (New Delhi: Vistar, 2005), 162.

44. Fred S. Siebert, Theodore Peterson, and Wilbur Schramm, *Four Theories of the Press* (Chicago: University of Illinois Press, 1963), 1.

45. Baran and Davis, *Mass Communication Theory*; McQuail, *McQuail's Mass Communication Theory.*

46. McQuail, *McQuail's Mass Communication Theory*, 171.

47. Ibid.

48. Baran and Davis, *Mass Communication Theory*, 99.

49. Uche, "Ideology, Theory and Professionalism," 1–16.

50. Ibid.

51. Stella Orakwue, "Africa—The World's Comfort Zone," *New African* (July–August 2001): 38.

52. Umaru A. Pate, "Strengthening Media Capacity for Investigative Journalism through Institutions' Based Curriculum" (paper presented at "News, Accountability and Strengthening Nigeria's Democracy" conference, Lagos, Nigeria, December 28, 2007).

53. Okigbo, quoted in Joseph O. Faniran, *Foundations of African Communication with Examples from Yoruba Culture* (Ibadan: Spectrum Books, 2008).

54. Faniran, *Foundations of African Communication.*

55. UNESCO Series on Journalism Education, *Model Curricula for Journalism Education for Developing Countries and Emerging Democracies* (Paris: UNESCO Communication, 2007), 6.

56. Ibid., 6, emphasis added.

57. Ibid., 7.

58. McBride, *Many Voices.*

59. Sadig Rasheed, "Africa at the Doorstep of the Twenty-First Century: Can Crisis Turn to Opportunity?" in *Africa Within the World: Beyond Dispossession and Dependence*, ed. Adebayo Adedeji (New York: Zed, 1993), 56.

60. Ibid., 58.

The African Renaissance and Discourse Ownership

Challenging Debilitating Discourses on Africa

Steve Odero Ouma

Introduction

Africa in the twenty-first century has experienced significant changes and advances toward realizing the African Renaissance. In comparison to the immediate postindependence period of the late 1980s and early 1990s when political instability was the norm, today Africa is without a doubt more peaceful. During these periods there were more than twenty-one military coups in Africa, namely, in Algeria, Burundi, Congo-Brazzaville, Democratic Republic of Congo (formerly Zaire), Central African Republic, Dahomey, Ethiopia, Gabon, Gambia, Lesotho, Liberia, Libya, Mali, Niger, Nigeria, Senegal, Sierra Leone, Somalia, Sudan, Togo, Uganda, Burkina Faso (formerly Upper Volta), and Zanzibar. Aside from the significantly smaller coups and military regimes in place and the institution of formal democracies in the continent and an ongoing process of constitutional reform in a plethora of countries from Kenya to Ghana, the continent is a far cry from the tumultuous region it was twenty years ago. Additionally, regarding economic growth, the World Bank has reported that sub-Saharan Africa alone registered an average growth of 6 percent GDP for the first time in 2006, well above historic averages for both developed countries and all developing countries.[1]

Despite the global financial crisis, Africa registered an increased average growth rate of 6.2 percent in 2007 and a drop to 3 percent in 2008. This is against the backdrop of economies in developed nations in the Euro zone registering an average of −4.8 percent, with Italy recording negative economic growth rate of −2.6 percent, Belgium

−3.1 percent, and Germany −3.8 percent in January 2009.[2] Moreover, living standards in Africa have hit their highest mark in the last five years since independence. Foreign private capital flow into Africa amounted to $38 billion in 2006, a figure surpassing the inflow of foreign aid. Further, with the establishment of the African Union (AU), a more elaborate regional organization as compared to its predecessor, the Organization of African Unity (OAU), African countries have for the first time been able to assemble fairly effective military forces to serve as peacekeepers in troubled African regions such as Somalia and Sudan. These facts do not erase the reality that Africa still faces formidable challenges relating to poverty, good governance, and political and economic stability.

Despite these commendable achievements, the image of Africa and the African is forlornly pejorative internationally. Many people around the world today generally display an abhorrent lack of knowledge about Africa because although they have never visited Africa, they possess certain images about the continent that they believe to be true. These images are a product of predominantly Western media and its representations of the continent in television programs, movies, and the Internet, as well as in print media, including newspapers, magazines, journals, and books.[3]

The predominantly Western media is largely responsible for a systematic trend of misrepresenting Africa to the world. In the same manner that colonialism had a distortive effect on the psyche of the colonized and that this distortion continues to manifest itself in the lives of individuals in the postcolonial world, many sociologists, psychologists, psychiatrists, and psychoanalysts agree that when individuals are continuously fed a type of image or misrepresentation, the result is the congealing of the images to form stereotypes or generalizations.[4] These meta-contexts have framed perceptions about the continent in a vicious cycle that has spanned generations.[5] This cycle is perpetuated when children of a given generation are born into an environment in which these meta-contexts are already deeply entrenched in the social fabric, from education to entertainment. All through childhood nurturing to adulthood, a worldview is formed through this warped mental construction. Generalizations and stereotypes, once deeply entrenched in the minds of persons, invariably create conditions that engender explanatory constructs used to interpret events or evaluate behav-

iors, such as the cultural practices of Africans, rather than inquisitorial constructs seeking to investigate the reasons behind events
or certain behaviors.

This constant misrepresentation has led to warped perceptions of
Africans and Africa among Africans and the rest of the world. Some
of these perceptions, for example, can be as ridiculous as the belief
that many people in the continent are living Stone Age lifestyles in
caves and trees while clad in leaves, bark, and animal skins.[6] These
perceptions prevail, despite clear evidence of the existence of cities
and modern life in Africa, particularly through the work of the tour-
ism industry. "Mythically instigated evolutionary edicts of life having
begun in Africa, the Africa's propensity to backwardness and tomfool-
ery" continue to be portrayed in the media.

Some of the most prolific images of Africa include that of Africa as
a "dark continent" characterized by primeval irrationality, so-called
"tribal" anarchy, civil war, political instability, flagrant corruption,
incompetent leadership and managerial ineptitude, hunger, famine,
and starvation as well as rampant diseases, especially AIDS.[7] Africa
is seen as a homogeneous entity made up of uncivilized and heathen
peoples who are culturally, intellectually, politically, and technically
backward or inferior, who are incapable of governing themselves
and embracing democratic principles of governance. The African
continent is depicted as the "dependent Africa," "crisis-driven Africa," and "hopeless" or "pitiable Africa." Without exception, the images have been negative, sensationalizing the "dark" side of Africa.
These images of Africa strongly pervade Western media and are
advanced and entrenched by journalists, politicians, and even aca-
demics.

Given the debilitating effects of this negative portrayal, the continent is in dire need of justified good publicity. While responding to
this need, this chapter addresses prevalent negative discourses on the
African continent and its experiences and their negative impact on
the prospects of an African Renaissance; points at some of the omit-
ted descriptions of Africa so as to put in perspective the gravity of
these misrepresentations and their damaging effect on the quest for
realization of the African Renaissance; and recommends a vital measure that can transform the Renaissance project from an aspiration
to a reality. It concludes by suggesting in general and specific terms
a way forward.

Clarification of terms: The "African Renaissance," "West," and "Africa"

The African Renaissance (the Renaissance) refers to the idea of a revival or renewal of Africa. Some of the key elements of the Renaissance vision should include the following:

- The economic recovery of the African continent as a whole and the establishment of political democracy on the continent.
- The need to break neocolonial relations between Africa and the world's economic powers.
- The mobilization of the people of Africa to take their destiny into their own hands, thus preventing the continent's being a place for the attainment of geopolitical and strategic interests of the world's most powerful countries.
- Fast development of a people-driven and people-centered economic growth and development aimed at meeting the basic needs of the people.[8]

Former South African president Thabo Mbeki has been one of the most prominent advocates of this endeavor, having delivered several moving speeches on the importance of realizing such a renaissance.[9] Various projects aimed at bringing about Africa's much-needed transformation have been established following these calls, for example, the New Partnership for Africa's Development (NEPAD) and the African Charter on Democracy, Elections and Governance.[10]

"The West" is a convenient shorthand term usually used to refer to Western Europe, North America, and regions that are predominantly populated by European settlers. "The West" not only refers to a particular geographic region but is also frequently associated with other qualities, such as the rule of law, representative government, capitalist (free market) economy, and the guarantee of certain rights and liberties, consumerism, liberalism, and individualism. Thus, the term "the West" refers to a geographical region as well as to the characteristics and values that are seen as predominant in this region. Other related terms, such as "Western" and "Westernization," are frequently used to refer to the characteristics and values described above common in the West, rather than in the geographical region. In this sense it is not uncommon to encounter reference to Westernization of African cities or declarations that a particular ideology endorses Western values.

At this point, it must be stressed that the West is not a homogeneous entity. The values described above find expression variously in different states. Consequently, Western discourses on Africa are diverse in nature. This chapter, in examining prevalent discourses on Africa, mostly Western in origin, will refer to those discourses that are relatively common and have considerable influence in the West and the world, thereby referring to these as "prevalent Western discourses." Indeed, discourses reflecting the same views and assumptions as those discussed in this chapter may emanate from regions other than the West, and while the discourses under discussion in the article are predominantly Western, their views and assumptions may not be exclusively Western. The term "prevalent Western discourse" must be understood as referring to a discourse that is produced by a citizen of a Western state, that has relative influence in the West and the world, and that does not express an uncommon or rarely expressed perspective in the West.

The term "Africa" is employed in this study to refer to a geographical region (the African continent), and the term "African" to anything emerging from that region. A discourse on Africa is thus a discourse that has its focus on the African continent or any subregion. The term "African" has been used to refer to people whose ancestry can be traced to the African continent (such as African Americans), but in this article "African" will be used to name people and issues taking place on the African continent.

Anatomy of the Problem: The Power of the Media

The predominantly Western media have traditionally played a fundamental role in the democratization process across the world. The media are a powerful tool, a trait derived from their role in the dissemination of information to a vast audience. The capacity of media houses to shape perceptions of people all around the world and influence international politics is enormous because . . . explain. International media today are even more powerful and influential than they were decades ago because of technological advances that make it easier to relay information within seconds of its occurrence.

The media's sophisticated approach to creating the African image, shaping and reshaping it as is deemed fit, goes largely unchallenged by those directly affected for a variety of reasons, including the lack of political stability, economic means to rebut the miseducation that is so constant and belligerent to the African people. The negative impacts of these overly negative representations are so far-reaching that even African descendants, who have virtually no cultural competence, have joined the charade and actually contribute to the pejorative perception of Africa globally. This attitude, while disturbing, also abets the media's denigration of Africa. Sadly, many indigenous Euro-Africans and Afro-Americans have joined in this travesty of a beleaguered condemnation of Africa.[11]

An Overview of Some Prevalent Western Discourses on the African Situation

Ailing Africa

It is not uncommon for Western writers to adopt negative and denigrating metaphorical language in writing about the African situation, so that depicting Africa as a diseased patient in need of medical assistance is an image frequently used by Western writers when writing about the African situation. Salopek describes Africa as an "ailing continent" and speaks of the "sickening of Africa."[12] In a similar vein, Baker has written that many young democracies in Africa "show signs of ill-health," with some "having been wounded, fatally."[13] Simon identifies the "diagnoses and prescriptions for Africa's ills," while Sada speaks of "cette Afrique qui meurt" (this dying Africa).[14] Anderson describes Africa as a continent that seems "*to be dying from a combination of disease, ethnic hatred and corruption.*"[15] Other examples of the same imagery include one describing Africa as suffering from "economic malaise," and, according to Green, Ghana is the victim of a "continent-wide plague of economic crisis, political decay and incipient anarchy."[16]

Africa's description as a basket case has featured in several Western discourses. Morrow, for example, calls Africa "the basket case of the planet,"[17] while Russell, for his part, speaks of Africa as "a basket case of civil wars and sufferings." De Young warns that Africa's basket cases must not "be allowed to fester."[18] Bob Geldof, celebrity activist, TV presenter, and member of the Africa Progress Panel, which was launched in April 2007 as an independent authority on Africa to focus world leaders' attention on delivering their commitments to the continent, recently embarked on a trip touring Africa. Accompanied by TV cameras, Geldof was documenting that "War, Famine, Plague & Death are the Four Horsemen of the Apocalypse riding hard through the roads of Africa."[19]

Other descriptions, predominantly Western in origin, that imply Africa is stricken with some terrible disorder requiring skillful doctoring to restore it to health include the following: Michaels: "Job's continent";[20] Callaghy: "a voracious sinkhole";[21] Shillinger: a "festering ghetto of the global village";[22] and Morrow: "a sort of neo-postcolonial breakdown."[23] Africa is a "continent ravagé" (ravaged continent),[24] a "shattered continent"[25] with "battered states."[26] No wonder Africa is "unhappy,"[27] the "most miserable,"[28] and a continent descending into "hell and squalor"[29] or "sinking into an abyss."[30]

It is apparent from the foregoing that the purpose of much of the reporting and media description of Africa has been and continues to be not to meet the noble objective of reporting news or to engage in meaningful discourse, but rather to entertain Western and by extension world audiences. It sells to sensationalize reporting and discourse on Africa. Titles such as "Africa in Chaos" are catchy, whereas ones such as "Marked Developments in Africa" would be less attractive. What seems to matter is not what changes the continent is and has been going through, the welfare of the inhabitants, or their prospects for a better life, but rather the exploitation of some aspects of their realities, even if it means exaggeration, for monetary gain or other sinister motives.

An Inherently Sickly and Weak Continent

Several other discourses have depicted Africa as predisposed to sickness and weakness. Several writers, again predominantly Western in origin, have suggested that the African continent is weak and sickly *by nature*. According these writers, Africa has not simply had the misfortune of falling ill, but is characterized by an inclination to easily become diseased; it has some kind of weakness that makes it prone to various debilitating conditions. The *Economist* has asked, "Does Africa have some inherent flaw that keeps it backward and incapable of development? Some think so." The article continues on this theme, commenting that "Africa was weak before the Europeans touched its coasts," and that African societies "are distrustful and bad at organization."[31]

Such discourse is magnified in international media through news and/or reports that perpetually paint Africans as heathen peoples who thrive in backward traditions, practices, and superstitions, as well as weird, outdated, and repugnant rites, such as female "circumcision" (otherwise going by the euphemistic or politically correct terminology of "female genital mutilation"—FGM). There has been in the recent past a lot of hype and propaganda on FGM in the Western print and visual media, including the Internet, on the way "enlightened" teenage girls are refusing to undergo FGM in Kenya.[32] The manner in which the FGM question has been handled in the media fails to put that issue in the historical and cultural contexts of the specific communities where it is practiced. It is depicted as a wanton act of barbarism widely orchestrated on unwilling subjects. The picture is represented as if virtually all communities embrace this practice. Much as FGM is a significant and essential topic, especially in this era of HIV/AIDS, its extensive coverage at the expense of other equally important and constructive events smacks of systematically biased news coverage aimed at a particular image being conveyed of the continent.[33]

The depiction of Africa as inherently weak and sickly is usually implicit rather than clearly stated, possibly because this idea is not considered politically correct today. The pessimisms regarding postapartheid South Africa's prospects can be considered an example of an inference that Africa is inherently prone to debilitation. Numerous Western writers seem to consider South Africa as a "true" African state now that it is ruled by black Africans, and have begun questioning whether South Africa would become "just like the rest of Africa." Thompson warned that South Africa "may be following the downward trajectory of tropical Africa," while the *Economist* described some problems in South Africa, asking if they "represent the first skid down the slippery African slope, one which has oiled the failure of so many other countries."[34] In a similar vein, Kenny has spoken of South Africa "going down the drain like the rest of Africa."[35] The examples above illustrate not only the strength of the terminology used to illustrate the continent but the sensational tone that has come to characterize discourse on the continent.

Critically Appraising the Prevalent
Discourses on the African Situation

Aside from the outright negative depiction of Africa in the prevalent discourses already discussed, the West and the international community at large have simultaneously been represented as capable of bringing healing to ailing Africa. Consider Westlake, who has insisted that "help will be needed (in Africa) from the international community on a large scale";[36] Jaycox, who opines that Africa "needs increased support from the international community";[37] and Spence, who has asserted that Western governments "have a role to play in helping Africa."[38] Wright states that "with some help, Africa looks to a better future," and then discusses the role of international institutions in efforts to "aid Africa on the long journey to peace and prosperity."[39]

On a drearier note, Morrow asks, "What are we to do with black Africa. . . . Should the industrialized, moneyed nations allow Africa to drift further and further into the margins, into poverty, starvation, disease, war?"[40] The theme that runs throughout all of these discourses is that Africa will indeed drift further into poverty, starvation, and all sorts of other predicaments if the West does not step in to help. A similar theme in most of these Western discourses on Africa is that of Africa being "worse off" than it was under colonial rule. This proposition that Africa is at its most healthy when under the supervision of the West seems inevitable and cannot be avoided in such self-serving discourses. Take Jensen, for example, who says that "black Africa is worse off today than it was under colonial rule";[41] and Dynes, who has warned that if Africa continues its "downward spiral," it will soon be poorer than it was "in David Livingstone's time."[42]

By claiming that Africa would be better off if under Western rule, such discourses suggest that Africa is incapable of taking care of itself, and an ailing Africa requires the intervention of the capable and knowledgeable medical doctor Dr. West. All this discourse renders the immense importance of Africa to the developed world to be only in the vast amounts of natural resources it exports. For example, the mineral industry of Mozambique plays a significant role in the world's production of aluminum, beryllium, and tantalum. In 2006, Mozambique's share of the world's mine output of tantalum amounted to 6 percent; of beryllium, 5 percent; and of aluminum, 2 percent.[43]

Conventionally, this help has been conceived of in terms of monetary aid, thereby linking this aid to certain conditions and pressuring African states to introduce changes understood by the West to be necessary for Africa's long-term health, regardless of whether such changes are perceived as necessary by the African people themselves. Judging by these discourses, the West is portrayed as an adept doctor equipped with medicines that can cure Africa's maladies. What is wrong or right about these discourses? These discourses have noble foundations in that they seek to address the state of underdevelopment in Africa, but they not only defeat their original objective but also work to hamper any efforts toward emancipating the continent from its condition.

These discourses are problematic for the following reasons. First, by presenting Africa as an ailing continent, such discourses evoke a dichotomy of illness and health that associates Africa with illness and the West with health. Illness cannot be understood without considering its opposite, health. To be ill is to lack health, and to be healthy involves, at the very least, the absence of illness. When the depiction of Africa as ill is accompanied by the depiction of the West as the doctor who can heal Africa, there is a suggestion that whereas the African continent is characterized by infirmity, the West is characterized by health. A doctor must be in possession of health, as well as the knowledge of how to maintain that health, before the doctor can begin to assist patients.

Implicit in this medical metaphor is a suggestion that in becoming healthy, Africa will become more like the West as the West is shown to characterize and dispense health. Such discourses thus advocate Africa's increased assimilation with the West and do not consider the possibility neither of African health being fundamentally different from Western health nor of both the African and the Western situations being characterized by illness. Furthermore, these discourses exclude the possibility of Africa healing itself, or of Africa defining its own ideal of health. The latter point is the very essence of the decolonization process and the African Renaissance.

A second problem with such discourses regards the power relations suggested by the use of a doctor-patient metaphor. It is often perceived that the doctor-patient relationship is not a relationship of equals. The doctor has something that the patient needs, placing the doctor in a powerful position in relation to the patient. In this case, it is presumed that the doctor's refusal to see the patient will be detrimental to the patient but not to the doctor. However, the doctor needs the patient to sustain his practice. Therefore, imagery portraying Africa as an ailing patient requiring the help of Dr. West ought to suggest a similar asymmetry in power relations, but it seldom does. Africa is typically shown as requiring the West to bestow upon it much-needed assistance and expertise, while the West is under no obligation to do so. This kind of discourse emerges from a particular worldview, one that perceives Africa as in need of assistance and the West as the source of such assistance, and also acts to perpetuate this worldview by predicting doom and disaster for Africa in the absence of Western assistance.

However, the converse position is never discussed. If the doctor refuses to see the patient, his medical practice will inevitably suffer, if not collapse. In this vein, the West needs Africa just as much as Africa needs the West. Africa is the richest continent in the world in terms of natural resources, and the West has the highest rate of consumption of these resources. Thus, rather than being a relationship of unequals, the reality is that the West-Africa relationship is one of symbiosis, and can to a considerable degree be arguably described as one of parasitism, with the West being the largest consumer of Africa's resources and not giving back in a mutually beneficial manner.

Despite this being the reality, the impression created is that Africa is the world's burden. That it is a perpetual beggar that has contributed in the past and contributes little if anything to the contemporary world order. This impression has had and continues to have a devastating effect on African efforts for advancement on all fronts, including political, economic, and social ones. These efforts are hampered by an environment that repeatedly tells the African he has been no good, is no good, and will never be of any good. This environment is entrenched by a Western-dominated international media and educational curriculum, both within Africa and abroad, that builds this phenomenon that is so debilitating to the African continent. What, then, are the prospects for African decolonization and realization of the African Renaissance?

Into Action: Calling for a Pan-African Broadcaster as a Crucial Part of the African Renaissance

As has been discussed above, the images of Africa in the Western media are, by and large, images of negative misrepresentation. Whether this is a result of biased, unbalanced, and subjective reporting or a consequence of a new way of perceiving reality where a few corporate giants are creating commercialized representations of Africa in order to maintain their own businesses and ideological agendas is not the issue. The issue is that these representations are always focused on the negative, the awkward, the weird, and the absurd, as well as the wild and the exotic.[44] However, the fact remains that these images are not all that Africa is, and many of these images are not unique to Africa. The question then becomes: What must be done to correct this misrepresentation?

The move toward correcting this detrimental parody must emanate from Africa. An African initiative must aim to accurately represent the truth to Africa and the world. The time has come for the African continent to be represented for what it is: a haven of uniquely rich cultures, blessed with vast amounts of natural resources as well as formidable challenges still to be overcome so as to realize its full potential. Africa is not inferior or the globally insignificant other. Africa is not the world's burden or sick patient. It is time that the world knew that Angola is the world's third-largest custodian of uranium deposits, and that Ghana is considering nuclear energy to support its energy sector.

As a central part of the African Renaissance, this study calls for the creation of one major African Broadcasting Network (ABN) comprising the major media houses in selected African countries that enjoy a relative freedom of the press. In direct contrast to the immediate postindependence period, today a larger number of African countries have, to a considerable degree, freed their presses. This partial realization of freedom of the press ought not to hinder the realization of this project. The network, which will include an online outlet, can begin with media houses in those countries in which press freedom is somewhat guaranteed. As the momentum and the beneficial effects of this endeavor begin to materialize, it will be apparent that those countries not already part of the enterprise should join in the enterprise. By bringing together the major and considerably successful national media houses in the form of a merger, consortium, association, or shareholding capacity in a new outfit, whichever is deemed fit after consultations, this network ought to set out to primarily broadcast African news reports and documentaries with international reach to Africa and beyond. By so doing, the wheels of the African Renaissance project will have received the grease needed to be set in motion.

Indeed, the gist of the idea proposed in this chapter is not completely novel. In 2007, in a conference in Portugal of Middle Eastern broadcasters, an independent Pan-African Broadcaster planning a twenty-four-hour news and information channel proposed an "African voice for Africa and the rest of the world." Following this call, Amin, a Kenyan photojournalist and entrepreneur based in Nairobi, set in motion the first step toward the realization of this project in September 2008 in Nairobi with the launch of "A24."[45]

The channel's model for development is similar to that of the Al Jazeera network in Qatar. As well as providing news, A24's mission is to communicate relevant information about cross-border issues, especially health care, the environment, business, art, and music, without failing to address the continent's problems. A24 seeks to start off as a news agency for freelance photographers and television reporters from across Africa. Similar to Reuters, these freelancers will send their images to A24, and the agency in turn will market them to international broadcasters. The journalists will receive 60 percent of the sales price of their work and keep the copyright. A24 will be a recruiting tool for the network, which is hoped to be launched within a year if the agency proves successful. The freelancers who submit the best content to the agency will become bureau chiefs for the envisaged network.

The planners of these initiatives found a similar initiative put in place by the South African Broadcasting Corporation (SABC). SABC International was launched in 2007 and is the first news channel dedicated to reporting international news from an African perspective. SABC International was launched in pursuit of the African Renaissance. In addition to news bulletins, the channel features current affairs, investigative programs, and business news from around the globe, making it a laudable contribution to well-balanced reporting on Africa.

The relevance, significance, and centrality of effective and constructive media coverage are not restricted to simply representing Africa in a positive manner. Such media will inevitably contribute to the democratization and good governance process. Previously secretive governments would be compelled by the wave of press freedom and interconnectedness to become more transparent and open. Rather than Africans' reading overly negative reporting on the problems plaguing their continent, they will in similar media read about positive political and economic advancements. Intracontinental understanding and consequent political and economic contact would increase. Such a Pan-African broadcaster would help build and fortify solidarity between North, West, East, and Southern Africa.

Opportunities for factional media to incite violence, as in Rwanda in 1994, for example, would be more easily limited as the media will be operating within a regional framework and hence will be open to circumspection. This broadcaster will act as an alternative and not a challenge to established Western broadcasters, although, just as is or was the case with the Al Jazeera network, it is bound to be viewed as a threat by Western outlets. A Pan-African broadcaster that reaches out to the diaspora, as Al-Jazeera has,[46] would also produce positive economic and cultural influences, inviting greater participation from Africans outside the continent.

Conclusion

Africa has for far too long relied on others to tell it its own stories. This may sound like a lament about some dim and distant past, but it is the contemporary reality facing Africa and all its citizens. Because of the overly negative media coverage of Africa, Africans are afraid to sing their own songs and speak their native languages, and they are thoroughly intimidated to respect their cultures and honor their true heroes and heroines. Africans are rendered incapable of articulating their own reality and celebrating their achievements because through the international media, largely dominated by the Western media, they are relentlessly informed that their "many" setbacks, relative to their "virtually nonexistent" successes, should forever define their existence.

Not only is the African international broadcast-news landscape dominated by a few resource-rich channels predominantly of Western origin, but even when African broadcasters participate in the dissemination of news, it is always in the context of stories filed by foreign news agencies such as Reuters, with headquarters in Atlanta,

New York, London, and other major cities of the powerful nations.[47] Accordingly, a Pan-African broadcaster will tell African stories in as much depth and contextual detail as possible, physically traveling around the continent identifying the successes and reverses so as to reflect what is really happening. In this way, the work that this channel will produce would also provide a more balanced picture of the realities in all parts of the continent. The danger that needs to be guarded against is the broadcaster's becoming an African conduit of foreign views, stereotypes, and prejudices presented as facts. Rather than set up a news channel to broadcast on African affairs, which would in turn have to rely on foreign news agencies for its content, the broadcaster will, by creation of both a news agency and a channel of its own, seek to take possession of African discourses.

This broadcaster will serve as Africa's dependable mirror, reflecting to Africa and the rest of the world African actualities. Through its high-quality journalism, news-gathering operations, pursuit of truth, and correct contextualization of events and processes, the continent will be liberated from the half-truths and misrepresentations that have served to magnify a negative image of Africa. Africa will celebrate its many successes, such as the end of decades-old active conflicts in places such as Mozambique, Sierra Leone, Liberia, Angola, DR Congo, and Ivory Coast; as well as the entrenchment of democracy in countries such as Namibia and Ghana and Kenya; and the economic successes realized in Mauritius, Botswana, and Tunisia. Thus, celebration will ensue with proper coverage of successes on the continent rather than endless and distorted mourning about starving children with flies in their eyes, executions, and genocide. The good stories from Africa are indeed numerous and are proliferating by the day but lack an appropriate system to convey them to Africa and to the world, as well as a journalistic/media engine to advance them. The time is now!

Notes

1. William Easterly, "What Bono Doesn't Say about Africa," *Los Angeles Times*, July 6, 2007, http://www.latimes.com/news/opinion/la-oe easterly6jul06,0,6188154.story?coll=la-opinion-rightrail.

2. Trading Economics Global Economic Research, http://www.tradingeconomics.com/Economics/GDP-Growth.aspx?Symbol=EUR.

3. Easterly, "What Bono Doesn't Say."

4. Claude M Steele, "A Threat in the Air: How Stereotypes Shape Intellectual Identity and Performance," *American Psychologist* 52, no. 6 (1997): 613–29.

5. Thabo Mbeki, "Republic of South Africa Constitutional Bill 1996," accessed August 1, 2001, http://www.anc.org.za/ancdocs/history/mbeki/1996/960508.html; Christian S. Wheeler, Blair W. Jarvis, and Richard E. Petty, "Think unto Others: The Self-Destructive Impact of Negative Racial Stereotypes," *Journal of Experimental Social Psychology* 37 (2001): 173–80.

6. James Michira, "Images of Africa in the Western Media," December 23, 2002, http://www.teachingliterature.org/teachingliterature/pdf/multi/images_of_africa_michira.pdf.

7. Michira, "Images of Africa."

8. Mbeki, "Republic of South Africa."

9. Ibid.

10. African Charter on Democracy, Elections and Governance, www.africa-union.org/root/AU/Documents/Treaties/text/Charter%20on%20Democracy.pdf.

11. African, "The Prevalent Negative Portrayal of Africa in the International Media Smirks of Economic Malice," *Human Rights and Equity*, November 10, 2005, http://www.tigweb.org/express/panorama/article.html?ContentID=6561.

12. Paul Salopek, "Plagues of Old Reclaim Continent," *Chicago Tribune*, January 9, 2000, 1.

13. Bruce Baker, "Can Democracy in Africa Be Sustained?" *Commonwealth and Comparative Politics* 38, no. 3 (2000): 9–34.

14. Hugo Sada, "Une Livraison de 'Manière de Voir': Afriques en Renaissance," *Le Monde Diplomatique*, June 2000, 2.

15. J. Anderson, *End of an Era: France's Last Gasp in Africa* (Agentur: Deutsche Press, 1997).

16. Daniel Green, "Ghana: Structural Adjustment and State (Re)Formation," in *The African State at a Critical Juncture: Between Disintegration and Reconfiguration*, ed. Leonardo A. Villalon and Phillip A. Huxtable (Boulder, CO: Lynne Rienner, 1998), 185.

17. Lance Morrow, "Africa: The Scramble for Existence," *Time*, September 6, 1992, 25–37.

18. Karen DeYoung, "Generosity Shrinks in an Age of Prosperity," *Washington Post*, November 25, 1999, A1.

19. Easterly, "What Bono Doesn't Say."

20. Marguerite Michaels, "Retreat from Africa," *Foreign Affairs* 72, no. 1 (1993): 98–108.

21. Thomas M. Callaghy, "State, Choice, and Context: Comparative Reflections on Reform and Intractability," in *Political Development and the New Realism in Sub-Saharan Africa*, ed. David E. Apter and Carl G. Rosberg (Charlottesville: University Press of Virginia, 1994), 209.

22. Kurt Shillinger, "Africa's Strife Cools Investors' Ardor: Western Doubt Slows a Renaissance," *Boston Globe*, June 4, 2000, 8.

23. Morrow, "Africa."

24. Cécile Marin and Philippe Rekacewicz, "Afrique, Continent Ravagé," *Le Monde Diplomatique*, January 2000, www.mondediplomatique.fr/cartes/afriquemdv49.

25. Apter and Rosberg, "Changing African Perspectives," 43.

26. Christopher Clapham, "Democratization in Africa: Obstacles and Prospects," *Third World Quarterly* 14, no. 3 (1993): 423–38.

27. W. P. Hoar, "Darkness Covers a Continent," *New American* 8, no. 4 (1992): 41–48.

28. Morrow, "Africa."

29. Robert Fatton, "Liberal Democracy in Africa," *Political Science Quarterly* 105, no. 3 (1990): 455–73.

30. Michael Dynes, "Coming to Africa's Aid Has Been No Help," *Times*, November 23, 2000.

31. "Africa: The Heart of the Matter," *Economist*, May 13, 2000, 23–25.

32. Michira, "Images of Africa."

33. Ibid.

34. "Africa: The Heart of the Matter."

35. Andrew Kenny, "Dread and Jubilation Are Replaced by Gloom . . . and Stability," *Electronic Telegraph*, May 30, 1999, 1465.

36. M. Westlake, "Africa's Last Chance," *Focus* 110 (1989): 10–11.

37. E. V. Jaycox, "Sub-Saharan Africa: Development Performance and Prospects," *Journal of International Affairs* 46, no. 1 (1992): 81–95.

38. J. Spence, "Africa: What Does the Future Hold?" *Strategic Review for South Africa* 19, no. 2 (1997): 1–14.

39. F. Wright, "A Comeback in the Making," *Star Tribune* (Minneapolis, MN), October 13, 1996, 17A.

40. Morrow, "Africa."

41. H. Jensen, "For Africa, a New Millennium Does Not Mean a New Day," *Scripps Howard News Service*, September 1, 1999.

42. Dynes, "Coming to Africa's Aid."

43. Thomas R. Yager," "The Mineral Industry in Mozambique 2006," *Year Book of Minerals Mozambique*, http://minerals.usgs.gov/minerals/pubs/country/2006/myb3-2006-mz.pdf.

44. Michira, "Images of Africa."

45. "Kenya: Launch of A24 Media Revolutionises," African Media Environment Press Release, September 2008, accessed June 28, 2008, http://allafrica.com/stories/200809191032.html.

46. Mohammed el-Nawawy and Adel Iskandar, "Al-Jazeera: How the Free Arab News Network Scooped the World and Changed the Middle East," *Political Science Quarterly* 118, no. 3 (2003): 316–18.

47. Mbeki, "Republic of South Africa."

Part III

Decolonizing Knowledge:
Intellectual Imperatives and Epistemic Dialogues

Decolonization and the
Practice of Philosophy

Tsenay Serequeberhan

When the axe came into the forest, the trees said: the handle is one of us.

—Turkish proverb

What has been, to date, the character of African decolonization, and how is it related to the practice of philosophy? In engaging this double question what I hope to do, at least in outline, is to look at the actuality of decolonization as it has unfolded thus far, and examine the way in which philosophy—the metaphysical tradition of the West— has served as a theoretic buttress for colonialism. I will also look at how the contemporary practice of African philosophy can serve as a reflective supplement necessary for the consummation of Africa's ongoing decolonization, of which it is a rather late theoretic offshoot.[1] In this double effort, the focus will be on exploring the character and substance of *decolonization* and the responsibility this lived world-historical situation and process imposes on *us*—African *intellectuals*.

- I -

But first let us begin by looking at philosophy's own self-understanding. In his book *Vocazione e responsabilità del filosofo*, Gianni Vattimo points out that philosophical arguments are discourses aimed at "persuasion" and situated in the shared views of "a collectivity."[2] And so, he observes: "It becomes clear that it essentially concerns proposals for interpreting our common situation according to a certain line and starting from shared presuppositions."[3] In such "proposals" and deliberations we try to persuade one another by presenting arguments and citing authors we value and our counterparts in dialogue also value and appreciate. The authors we cite, furthermore, are not concerned with demonstrating that such and so is or is not the case, based on indisputable facts,[4] but are themselves engaged in persuading one another and searching for a shared interpretation of a "common situation,"[5] which has become—in view of lived exigencies and concerns—problematic and worthy of questioning. Our persuasiveness is therefore not merely a rhetorical ploy directed at others, but a critical and reflective exploration of the situation at hand directed not only, or primarily, at others, but more importantly, at ourselves.[6]

To validate our respective interpretations of the "common situation," we thus cite, to one another, interpreters and interpretations in whose esteem or appreciation we agree. From this it follows that the truth we try to maintain, and the way in which we maintain it, is along the lines of arguing for a stance, or a perspective, in view of certain accepted reference points, in terms of which we can then pose the critical question: "How can you still say this?"[7] In other words, asks Vattimo, "is it not perhaps true that the experience procured for you by a reading of Nietzsche (or of Kant, or of Hegel) impedes you from saying things that perhaps at one time you might have said and sustained?"[8] The question then is: Don't the insights secured in reading such and similar thinkers compel us to reconsider, or confirm, our thus-far-held prejudices and/or presuppositions?

The affirmative response to this rhetorical question takes for granted accord in our deeds and words,[9] and assumes rigor and consistency as indispensable for the practice of philosophy: a kind of reflection that incessantly assesses and reassesses itself, in light of "all that which happens in human reality."[10] Otherwise, the "How can you still say this?" of philosophy, as Socrates patiently explains to Crito, would be "in truth play and nonsense."[11] In all of this, our efforts are aimed at validating, and/or discarding, our prejudices or "shared presuppositions," and calibrating, accordingly, the line of sight that they make possible. Philosophy is therefore focused on sifting and exploring our presuppositions and prejudgments—the prejudices we live by[12]—in view of the shared possibilities of our present. Consequently, it stands in very close proximity to history; it is the reflectively critical self-validation of its lived time—its historicity.[13] Conversely, the historicity in which a philosophic discourse finds itself furnishes the problems of concern and concretely establishes the contextual background within and out of which a specific philosophic discourse fore-grounds its interpretations.[14]

Now, this self-understanding of philosophy is not a view that is pe-culiar, or idiosyncratic, to Vattimo. It is the basic self-comprehension of the practice of philosophy. As Hegel points out, for example, "Phi-losophy . . . is its own time apprehended in thoughts."[15] It is, in other words, the persuasive and critical-reflective exploration of the viable conceptions and ideas of its lived time. Similarly, Kant, referring to his own moment of time as "the age of criticism," notes that "everything must submit" to critical scrutiny and be "able to sustain the test of a free and open examination,"[16] which is, properly speaking, the practice of philosophy. This, too, is what Nietzsche means, *grosso modo*, when he states that "this art of transfiguration *is* philosophy."[17]

- II -

This critical, persuasive, and reflectively transfigurative engagement with, and apprehension of, the actuality of what is—the interpretative practice of philosophy—constituted as the metaphysical tradition of the West, the highest and most sublime realm of European culture, has served, for the longest time, as the reflective-theoretic prop for the practice of colonialism. Just as, at one time, philosophy was the handmaid of theology, at a later date, when it secured employment with science, it concurrently became the attendant of expansion and conquest. In keeping with European modernity's progressive self-understanding—in its agonistic encounter of the perceived regressive actuality of the rest of the globe—philosophy mapped out the meta-physical presuppositions of this attitude. As Anne Hugon points out:

> In 1788 [i.e., the heyday of the Enlightenment] a booklet was issued in London by the newly formed Association for Promoting the Discovery of the Interior parts of Africa (or the African Association). It stated [at its founding] that at least one third of the inhabited surface of the earth was un-known, notably Africa, virtually in its entirety. For the first time this ignorance was seen as a shameful gap in human knowledge that must immediately be filled.[18]

It was in light of this newly noticed "shameful gap," and to remedy this shortfall in "human knowledge," that the Association advocated for the discovery of the "interior parts of Africa." There is here, it should be noted, a seamless confluence in the pursuit of knowledge and the conquest of Africa and the world beyond Europe. Internal to this pursuit, furthermore, is a circular self-validation of what the "interior parts of Africa" showed themselves to be and what Europe expected and found in these supposed remote regions—in view of its own self-flattering perception of itself. And so, armed with this self-righteous stance, as Romano Guardini tells us: "For the new man of the modern age the unexplored regions of his world were a challenge to meet and conquer. Within himself he heard the call to venture over what seemed an endless earth, to [effectively] make himself its master."[19]

Europe's expansion, fueled by the politico-economic dynamism of ascending capitalist energies, found scientific legitimation in the enlightened effort to overcome "this ignorance," which was felt "for the first time" as a "shameful gap in human knowledge." In this, the clarion call of the Enlightenment, *Sapere aude* (Dare to know) was itself, beyond the otherworldly concerns of the medieval past, a motivating factor of conquest, mastery, and knowledge. The "man of the modern age" saw the world as "his" and in this new vision, empowered by this worldly orientation, resolved to make tangible its control. Enveloped and encouraged by this vista, the vigorous politico-economic dynamism of an ascending capitalism instituted a paradigm shift that enabled, and indeed embraced, colonial expansion.[20]

But before going on to see how philosophy renders service by supplying the metaphysical anchoring-stones for this bracing, it is necessary to first take a quick glance at the "pretext" that directs and gears the implementation of this project.[21] In other words, to look at how the progressive self-understanding of Europe appears to itself— and is presented to others—as an effort focused on the improvement of humanity, while engaged in its systematic subjection. We need to see how Europe's enlightened orientation, in its global projection, is transmuted into violent conquest—to see, concretely, what is *muted* in this change.

- III -

Modern European colonialism—the subjection of non-European peoples designated as inferior and primitive, and their transformation for their own improvement and welfare—was grounded on, and derived its legitimacy from, a rather stuck-up and imperious altruism. For the longest time, this violent benevolence saw itself as the proper embodiment and manifestation of the humanity of the human in intercultural relations. A certain group of human beings, notably those with a lighter complexion, believed themselves to have possession of the *true God* and to have discovered *the proper way* of organizing human life on earth; and so they felt compelled to civilize the rest of humanity—to make it like themselves—and share their blessings. In other words, as Father Placide Temples, a missionary priest, points out: "It has been said that our civilizing mission alone can justify our occupation of the lands of uncivilized peoples."[22]

European colonial expansion saw and presented itself as the actuality, in actualization, of the normatively proper relation among human beings, ranked in a hierarchy of subordination. In this context colonial subjection was seen—its harshness and violence notwithstanding—as a benevolent act with long-term beneficial effects, directed toward the darker, less fortunate, and uncivilized backward peoples of the world. As Edward W. Said has observed:

> What distinguishes earlier empires, like the Roman or the Spanish or the Arabs, from the modern [colonial] empires, of which the British and French were the great ones in the nineteenth century, is the fact that the latter ones are systematic enterprises, constantly reinvested. They're not simply arriving in a country, looting it and then leaving when the loot is exhausted. . . . Modern empire requires . . . an idea of service, an idea of sacrifice, an idea of redemption. Out of this you get these great, massively reinforced notions of, for example, in the case of France, the *"mission civilisatrice."* That we're not there to benefit ourselves, we're there for the sake of the natives.[23]

It was under the guise and mantle of such an *idea* that by the end of the nineteenth century the dismemberment and partitioning of Africa, among the Christian powers of Europe, was completed. In shouldering its responsibility to the rest of us—"The White Man's Burden,"[24] Rudyard Kipling's memorable phrase—Europe globalized itself. In doing so, as Said further points out, it generously utilized force, "but much more important . . . than force . . . was the idea inculcated in the minds of the people being colonized that it was their destiny to be ruled by the West."[25]

The period of colonial rule, utilizing a violent pedagogy[26]—the strenuous and stern work of missionaries and altruistic educators—firmly entrenched, in the colonized, the necessity for this destiny. It hammered into their heads the idea of Western supremacy. In so doing, it originated a stratum, or layer, of people—Westernized Africans[27]—that, having been formed by Europe's imperious gaze, understand themselves and their place in the world in these terms. Europe converted those sections of the subjected it westernized to the view that their subjection was a necessity if their territories were to progress and develop and become places of civilized human habitation. In doing so, it firmly ingrained in their consciousness—subliminally and explicitly—the civilized-uncivilized dichotomy and persuaded them of their shortfall, within the scope of this all-engulfing distinction.[28] And so, as Basil Davidson points out: "Most Africans in Western-educated groups . . . held to the liberal Victorian vision of civilization kindling its light from one new nation to the next, [and] drawing each within its blessed fold, long after the local facts depicted a very different prospect."[29]

Having accepted the self-proclaimed European civilizing idea, in 1901, for example, Angolans living in Lisbon published a protest against Portuguese misrule of their country. They noted that "Portugal had conquered Angola centuries earlier . . . but [had] done nothing for the people's welfare." To this day, "'the people remain brutalized, as in their former state,' and such neglect was an 'outrage against civilization.'"[30] In the above, it is implicitly understood and explicitly conceded that precolonial Africa was immersed in a condition of utter darkness. This is the operative internalized "pretext"—the disappointed expectation of beneficial effects to be secured from European rule, by the rightly conquered backward society—that explicitly condones and excuses conquest. This, then, is the consenting to, or accepting, the "pretext" of the *idea*—the "ideological pacification"[31] of the colonized: the tangible intellectual-cultural correlate to military-political pacification, which inaugurates the presence of Europe in Africa.[32]

What this does is to render the formerly colonized, who have internalized the colonial model of human existence and history, into permanent supplementary appendages of the West. Such persons, grounded not in an indigenous history or tradition but in the vestiges of imperial Europe, have as the yardstick of their existence an exteriority that has to be constantly emulated. This is the source of the extroversion of Westernized Africa, noted by Frantz Fanon in *Les damnés de la terre,* as the worship of the "Greco-Latin pedestal."[33] Existence for such persons is an ongoing process of self-nullification. Like Kafka's ape, biological life is sustained by the never-ending nullification of its indigenous ethical-historical ground. But what exactly does this mean? Let us, by way of an illustration, look at a noted and emblematic example of such a case.

Léopold Sédar Senghor, writing in 1961—one year after the "Year of Africa"—ardently affirms: "Let us cease vituperating colonialism and Europe. . . . Of course, the conquerors disseminated ruin in their path, but also ideas and techniques."[34] But what exactly does this mean? Senghor explains in great detail:

> When placed . . . in context, colonization will appear to us as a necessary evil, a historical necessity whence good will emerge, but on the sole condition that we, the colonized of yesterday, become conscious and that we will it. Slavery, feudalism, capitalism, and colonialism are the successive parturitions of History, painful like all parturitions. With the difference that here the child suffers more than the mother. That does not matter. If we are fully conscious of the scope of the *Advent,* we shall . . . be more attentive to contributions than defects, to possibilities of rebirth rather than to death and destruction. Without . . . European depredations, no doubt . . . Negro Africans . . . would by now have created more ripe and more succulent fruits. I doubt that they would have caught up so soon with the advances caused in Europe by the Renaissance. The evil of colonization is less these ruptures than that we were deprived of the freedom to choose those European contributions most appropriate to our spirit.[35]

What speaks in and through Senghor is the stern educational-cultural formation of the colonial period, whose destructive effects are here presented, by a brilliant pupil, as the conditions of the possibility for future beneficial effects—provided that "we, the colonized of yesterday, become conscious" that to secure "the advances caused in Europe by the Renaissance," such "death and destruction" was necessary. If only that were the case! Indeed, as Julius K. Nyerere tells us:

> At independence, Tanzania or as it was then called, Tanganyika (a country four times the size of Great Britain) had

approximately 200 miles of tarmac road, and its "industrial sector" consisted of six factories—including one which employed 50 persons. The countries which had sizeable Settler or mineral extraction communities (such as Kenya, Zimbabwe, Zambia or Congo) had strong links with the world economy, but their own development was entirely concentrated on servicing the needs of the settlers or the miners in one way or another. Again . . . at independence less than 50% of Tanzanian children went to school—and then for only four years or less; [and] 85% of its adults were illiterate in any language. The country had only two African engineers, 12 Doctors, and perhaps 30 Arts graduates.[36]

This can hardly be considered catching up with "the advances caused in Europe by the Renaissance"! Furthermore, in view of the massiveness of the destruction caused by colonial conquest, one could respond to Senghor by repeating Albert Memmi's rhetorical question: "How can one dare compare the advantages and disadvantages of colonization? What advantages, even if a thousand times more important, could make such internal and external catastrophes acceptable?"[37]

But beyond Memmi's rhetorical question, and Nyerere's marshaling of evidence, it is necessary to note that Senghor's way of "seeing" falls squarely within the confines of the "idea of service" that informs and directs colonial conquest. In his use of the childhood metaphor, in his endorsement of suffering in order to secure future benefits, in his view that colonialism is "a historical necessity whence good will emerge," in advising attentiveness to colonial contributions without even decrying all that Africa lost in being enslaved and colonized, in his eagerness to "choose" from "European contributions"—in all of this—Senghor replicates, as his own, the language of colonialism: the language of "the idea of service."

It is important to note that this "idea of service" and "of sacrifice," this "idea of redemption," aimed at saving and civilizing those seen as "half devil and half child,"[38] finds its ultimate source in the narratives of human progress, emancipation, and salvation, which derive from the Age of Enlightenment. It is necessary to note further that the persuasiveness of these overlapping narratives—of humanity ascending to light, freedom, and deliverance—presuppose, and indeed require, a rather dastardly and dark *image* of a past from which humanity is seen as ascending. In the context of Europe, the medieval past played this role,[39] the same role assigned to precolonial Africa by the "pretext" of the idea.

Indeed, as Chinua Achebe has noted, there is "a four-hundred-year period, from the sixteenth century to the twentieth," of abusive writing on Africa that has "developed into a tradition with a vast storehouse of lurid images to which writers went again and again through the centuries to draw 'material' for their books."[40] This, then, is the systematic deployment of the sedimented and layered conceptions and negative images—of "facts"—that "for the new man of the modern age," as we noted earlier with Guardini, comprised the actuality of Africa.[41] This writing articulates the images and consolidates the ordinary notions and conceptions of Africa as a land of heathens in need of civilizing conquest. This, then, was, and still is today, the "normal discourse"[42] of what Said refers to as "the epistemology of imperialism."[43]

It is imperative to note that this "epistemology of imperialism" finds its ultimate source and authorization—its metaphysical anchoring-stones—in the thinking of the icons of the modern tradition of European philosophy. The great minds of this tradition—including Locke, Hobbes, Hume, Kant, Hegel, and Marx—all had access to, and utilized, this "storehouse of lurid images." In articulating their differing outlooks, they streamlined the derogatory claims of this "storehouse" and gave it currency. They did so by articulating the *idea* and giving metaphysical backing to the supposed empirical descriptions of Africa—and the non-European world—that were, and still are, circuitously validated by their own speculative efforts.[44]

And so, behind the many and varied perspectives that constitute the philosophical tradition of the West, one finds the singular view—a core grounding axiom—that European modernity is, properly speaking, isomorphic with the humanity of the human per se. Stripped of its narcissism, as Vattimo points out, this banality affirms that: "we Europeans are the best kind of humanity [*noi europei siamo la migliore forma di umanita*], the whole course of history is ordered so as to realize more or less completely this ideal [incarnated in us]."[45] This, then, is the idealization of Europe's *idea* of itself—the service rendered colonialism by philosophy. Indeed, a lofty and disinterested task!

In this double game,[46] the West is both the ideal and its concrete historical instantiation. The great minds of the West, in idealizing their own history, fabricated the metaphysical *idea* in whose name colonial conquest was authorized. This is the same idea, as noted earlier with Davidson, that Westernized Africa was made to internalize. The very one that directs the logic of Senghor's considered pronouncements. It is in this context, then, that we need now to ask the question of what the contributions of African philosophy can be—in the present situation.

- IV -

Armed with its own sense of self, in political and armed confrontation, Africa ended direct colonial rule starting in the late 1950s. It is important to remember that, at the time, this was not something that was given universal acclaim.[47] It was therefore against tremendous odds that, bit by bit, formal independence was secured. In this, Africa, along with the rest of the colonized world that up to then had been excluded from history, reinserted itself into the actuality of human historical existence. Writing in 1958, for example, Fanon observed: "The XXth century, on the scale of the world, will not only be the era of atomic discoveries and interplanetary explorations. The second upheaval of this epoch and incontestably, is the conquest by the peoples of lands that belong to them."[48]

And yet, when we look back we see not only great achievements but also great disappointments. When we look at "all that which" has happened in "human reality" since the days of Fanon, we see the formerly colonized—under various guises and new modalities—being recolonized.[49] For though the formerly colonized have indeed reclaimed the "lands that belong to them," in large measure *we*, however, have failed to reclaim ourselves and take control of our own historical existence. More than in Asia, or Latin America, this is especially true of postcolonial Africa. As one of Sembène Ousmane's tragicomic characters confesses, in a lucid moment of angst: "We are nothing better than crabs in a basket. We want the ex-occupiers place? We have it. . . . Yet what change is there really in general or in particular? The colonialist is stronger, more powerful than ever before, hidden *inside us*, here in this very place."[50]

This is our contemporary inheritance. How then do we purge the colonial residue that still controls—from within—the actuality of the present? As we noted earlier, in reference to Senghor, this is the residue of colonial Europe's sense of history and human existence. It is this internalized *idea* that today directs the thinking of those who rule Africa. That this *idea*—of Europe serving, sacrificing for, and redeeming the darker and inferior portions of humanity—is false is today something that does not require much argument.[51] And yet, to date, the implicit prejudices (prejudgments), the salient and unspoken "shared presuppositions" that authorized it, are still with us.

As noted earlier with Vattimo, philosophy is a discourse that critically and persuasively aims to explore and engage our shared prejudices and presuppositions, in light of the exigencies of our lived "common situation." In this, as Hans-Georg Gadamer has remarked, "philosophical thinking simply consists in making what we already know another step more conscious."[52] In our context, this is the task of what I have named "the critical-negative aspect of the discourse of contemporary African philosophy."[53] The critical exploring and exposing of the "shared presuppositions" of "our common situation"—a *situation* in which the physical presence of colonial rule has ended, and yet, the *ideas* and *concepts* that structured and sanctioned it still endure. To make "more conscious" here means to destructure the symmetry of images, ideas, and concepts that today, as in the past, underlie Western hegemony.

This critical-negative project, as I have argued elsewhere, is a crucial component of intellectual decolonization. For in spite of the fact that colonialism has ended, its cultural and intellectual residue still endures and is utilized to perpetuate the political-economic submission of the formerly colonized. Intellectual "housecleaning" is thus an indispensable supplement necessary for the completion of our political self-liberation. Just as the political and armed struggle ended the de facto actuality of colonialism, the critical-negative project of African philosophy has to challenge and undo the de jure philosophic underpinnings that justified this now defunct actuality and still today sanction Western hegemony. And this, by extension, is applicable *grosso modo*, to all intellectual work on Africa.

In this regard, African philosophy can serve as a juncture for the differing discourses on Africa. To the extent that philosophy—which unlike the other disciplines does not have a sectional and specified domain—is concerned with exploring the sense of what *is*, it can serve as a reference point for our various intellectual undertakings. In all of this, what has to be kept in mind is that the demise of colonialism by force of arms and political confrontation has to be not merely the ending of the balance of physical force that made it possible, but also the termination of the hubris that gave it intellectual and moral currency. In agreement with Rousseau, one has to recognize that force, for or against colonialism, does not and cannot bestow political, or moral, sanction on its effects. Such endorsement, as in the past, is the task of intellectual reflection, the systematic querying of our "common [con-temporary] situation."

In our present postcolonial world, it is imperative to note that our former colonizers, the Western powers, occupy a dominant position not merely through "the force of" their "weapons" but, much more importantly, through the "'models' of growth and development" that they espouse and which "are today adopted everywhere."[54] For, colonization did not merely destroy the modes of life through which pre-colonial Africa lived its existence. In destroying precolonial Africa, it constituted colonized Africa as a dependent appendage of a Eurocentric world in all spheres of life. In doing so, it concurrently established the intellectual parameters, the "models of growth and development" that are operative in, and determine, the actuality of the present.

Within this array of systematically deployed understandings and of methodically amassed knowledge—in and through which humanity interpretatively comprehends itself and regulates its relation with the natural environment—within the symmetry of concepts, models, ideas, and interpretations, that constitutes this web of knowledge: to the "vast storehouse of lurid images," has been added the actuality of a dysfunctional continent that is incapable of doing for itself. In this way the myth of an inherently impaired darker sector of humanity has been born. And the daily news on Africa—genocide, man-made famine, corruption, female genital mutilation, and so on—substantiates this image, or *idea*, of a continent wedded to perdition.[55]

In all of this, what is lost sight of is the fact that Africa today, in spite of its independence, is a continent—on the whole—still indirectly controlled by its former colonizers. For example, as Martin Plaut, a BBC Africa analyst, points out:

> Driving round many African cities one is constantly struck by the blue and white of the UN flags and logos. . . . Frequently one is left with the impression that UN officials know at least as much, if not more, about [African] countries than [African] government ministers, many of whom spend more time nursing their political careers than their constituents. It is hard to escape the conclusion that if Af-

rica is not being re-colonized by the UN, then it is certainly being run at least as much from New York as it is from most of the continent's capitals.[56]

Not rooted in local conditions, the ministers and ministries of African governments are held in place by foreign props lubricated by graft.[57] Thus, "corruption," as Elizabeth Blunt, another BBC Africa analyst, points out, "is costing the continent nearly $150bn a year."[58] To be sure, there is nothing new in all of this. As Fanon noted, at the dawn of African independence, without eradicating the long-term effects of colonial rule and radically restructuring the actuality of independence—to the measure of what it names—independence is nothing more than "a minimum of re-adaptation, some reforms at the summit [of power], a flag and, down below, the undivided mass, forever 'medievalized,' which continues its perpetual [nervous] movement."[59]

To date, and on the whole, this is the actuality of independent Africa. Each African state has a flag that marks the geographic terrain within which specified Westernized elites (Francophone, Anglophone, etc.) live colonial lifestyles—at the expense of the vast majority—with the implicit and explicit encouragement and financial-military backing of our former colonizers.[60]

As Edward Said has noted, "In effect this really means that just to be an independent postcolonial Arab, or black [African], or Indonesian is not a program, nor a process, nor a vision. It is no more than a convenient starting point from which the real work, the hard work, might begin."[61]

Independence, which should have been "a convenient starting point," was taken as the final moment of Africa reclaiming itself. The "real work, the hard work" subsequent to the formal ending of colonial rule, of economic and political restructuring and rethinking the character and substance of independence, was never undertaken. In lieu of this "hard work," a caste of westernized Africans was established in power, and "*cette caste*," as Fanon points out, "has done nothing other than to take over unchanged the legacy of the economy, the thought, and the institutions left by the colonialists."[62] It is this "legacy" that today rules postcolonial Africa.

In view of all of the above and in the context of African philosophy, "the real work, the hard work," that Said points to is the systematic critique of this "legacy" on the level of ideas, aimed at seeing beyond the "models of growth and development" that mask and sustain dominance.[63] For it is through ideas and concepts that the legacy of colonialism rules the present. This "real work," then, is, on the one hand, the systematic critique of the Occidental tradition that sustains these "models," and on the other hand, a systematic sifting through traditions—European and African—aimed at synthesis.

This is what Amílcar Cabral referred to as "a selective analysis of the values of the culture within the framework" of our needs and exigencies.[64] It is in this way that we can properly engage our contemporary situation and further advance the ongoing decolonization of Africa. The aim in all of this is not to reject the West, nor merely to embrace our African traditions, but to cultivate and develop a concrete synthesis—in view of the contemporary situation. In this the concern of our philosophic reflections will not be *authenticity*, à la Senghor, but the *pragmatic utility* of the cultural-historical resources that constitute our mixed heritage. The task and responsibility of African philosophy, and of intellectual work focused on Africa, is thus an ongoing conceptual purging of all that was imposed on us.

In this effort, the aim is to bypass the residual remnants of our colonial past—make them irrelevant—by concretely undermining the "models" and "shared presuppositions" that sustain our deplorable present. This is also, and concurrently, an engaged exploring of the possibilities of our hybrid heritage. The importance of all of this lies in the fact that, at the end of the day, the only thing that really matters in our philosophic explorations is the character of the lived existence we strive toward and help to bring about. For, as Herbert Marcuse has pointedly observed, what we have today

> is not the old colonialism and imperialism (although in some aspects, the contrast has been overdrawn: [for] there is little essential difference between a direct government by the metropolitan power, and a native government which functions only by grace of a metropolitan power). The objective rationale for the global struggle is not the need for immediate capital export, resources, [or] surplus exploitation. It is rather the danger of subversion of the established hierarchy of Master and Servant, Top and Bottom, a hierarchy which has created and sustained the have-nations, Capitalist *and* Communist.[65]

At present, we need not worry about "actually existing socialism"; it has been swept away into *the dustbin of history* (ironically, a favorite phrase of its proponents) by its internal contradictions overdetermined by the Cold War. What remains are the "have-nations" of the capitalist West, which, under the leadership of the USA—the guise or cloak of democracy, good-governance, development aid, regional-global stability, the war on terror, and so on; and many (always changing!) other guises—aim to keep the "hierarchy of . . . Top and Bottom" in place. The challenge for philosophy—for that discourse that incessantly assesses itself in light of "all that which happens in human reality" and goes on, and on, about "how can you still say this?"—is to persuasively think through the avenues for subverting this *hierarchy*: on the level of ideas.

This, then, is the task of the "critical-negative aspect of the discourse of contemporary African philosophy," the task of rendering theoretic service to Africa's ongoing decolonization. Within the parameters of our respective disciplines, this is a crucial intellectual undertaking for those of us concerned with Africa. For as intellectuals—African or otherwise—working within the domains of various disciplines, the responsibility that we have is to make our respective scholarly projects concrete undertakings aimed at human betterment.

Notes

Epigraph: As quoted by Gérard Chaliand in the exordium to *Revolution in the Third World* (New York: Viking, 1977).

1. Theophilus Okere, *African Philosophy: A Historico-Hermeneutical Investigation of the Conditions of Its Possibility* (Lanham, MD: University Press of America, 1983), vii.

2. Gianni Vattimo, *Vocazione e responsabilità del filosofo* (Genoa: Il Melangolo, 2000), 71.

3. Ibid.

4. As Vattimo puts it: "I try to persuade you citing authors that I know you have also read and experienced, who were not in their turn demonstrating that 2+2 is 4 [i quali a loro volta non dimonstravano propriamente che 2+2 fa 4], but were seeking for *an interpretation of the common situation*." Ibid., 71. What is in question, then, are not conceptions and ideas internal to an accepted tradition—a "normal science" exchange of ideas focused on rigor—but a situation of "extraordinary science" in which ideas between traditions, or in a tradition in crisis, are being assessed in an effort to sift out possible avenues of exit from the crisis that can possibly institute, or lead to, a new paradigm. This is the basic idea that Vattimo is suggesting,

an idea that Thomas S. Kuhn in, *The Structure of Scientific Revolutions* (Chicago: University of Chicago Press, 1970), articulated, systematically, within the parameters of the history and philosophy of science.

It is important to note that this is the regular state of affairs in philosophic discourse that has not been reduced to an ideological profession of faith (i.e., a worldview). In other words, as Drew A. Hyland points out in *The Virtue of Philosophy: An Interpretation of Plato's* Charmides (Athens: Ohio University Press, 1981), the proper vocation of philosophy is to cultivate this openness to possibilities, sustained by ongoing questioning in full recognition of our finitude, our lived horizon. In this perspective, "the facts" are nothing more than the accepted interpretations, or understandings, of what "is"—knowledge—that has sedimented as such; as a heritage or tradition.

Interesting discussions, in philosophy as in other fields, occur when these "facts" (i.e., the accepted interpretations of the *is-ness* of what is) become worthy of questioning. In this regard it ought to be noted that the word "fact" does not name something immutable and fixed for all time, for it derives from the "Latin *factum*, from neuter of *factus*, past participle of *facere*, to do or make." And so, "a fact" is something, done or made, and understood or interpreted in the way designated. This, however, does not mean that it is immutable and/or not open to further inquiry and/or interpretation and understanding as to what it is. Merriam-Webster Unabridged, s.v. "fact," http://unabridged.merriam-webster.com/cgi-bin/unabridged?va=fact&x=22&y=10.

5. Vattimo, *Vocazione e responsabilità*, 71.

6. This is how Socrates makes this point in the *Phaedo*:
I am in danger at this moment of not having a philosophical attitude about this, but like those who are quite uneducated, I am eager to get the better of you in argument, for the uneducated, when they engage in argument about anything, give no thought to the truth about the subject of discussion but are only eager that those present will accept the position they have set forth. I differ from them only to this extent: I shall not be eager to get the agreement of those present that what I say is true, except incidentally, but I shall be very eager that I should myself be thoroughly convinced that things are so.
Plato: Five Dialogues, trans. G. M. A. Grube (Indianapolis, IN: Hackett, 1981), 91a–b.

7. Vattimo, *Vocazione e responsabilità*, 72.

8. Ibid.

9. On this point, see Hans-Georg Gadamer, *Dialogue and Dialectic*, trans. P. Christopher Smith (New Haven, CT: Yale University Press,

1980); the chapter *"Logos* and *Ergon* in Plato's *Lysis"* is an exploration of this point; see specifically pp. 1–2 and 6.

10. Vattimo, *Vocazione e responsabilità*, 52. This is akin to Antonio Gramsci's conception of philosophy as an in-depth exploration of the traces of life that constitute our existence and have collected/sedimented without the benefit of an inventory. On this, see *Quaderni Del Carcere*, critical edition prepared by Valentino Gerratana for the Gramsci Institute, vol. 2 (Torino, Italy: Giulio Einaudi, 1975), 1375–78.

11. In full this is what Socrates says: "Or was that well-spoken before the necessity to die came upon me, but now it is clear that this was said in vain for the sake of argument, that it was in truth play and nonsense?" From *Crito*, in *Plato: Five Dialogues*, 46:d.

12. See Hans-Georg Gadamer, *Truth and Method* (New York: Crossroad, 1982), 245–73.

13. This is what Antonio Gramsci means when he states that philosophy and history form a block.

14. For an exploration of this point, see Marcien Towa, "Conditions for the Affirmation of a Modern African Philosophical Thought," in *African Philosophy: The Essential Readings*, ed. Tsenay Serequeberhan (New York: Paragon House, 1991), 187–200.

15. Friedrich Hegel, *Hegel's Philosophy of Right*, trans. T. M. Knox (New York: Oxford University Press), 11.

16. Immanuel Kant, *Critique of Pure Reason*, trans. N. K. Smith (New York: St. Martin's Press, 1965), 9.

17. Friedrich Nietzsche, *The Gay Science*, trans. Walter Kaufman (New York: Vintage Books, 1974), 35.

18. Anne Hugon, *The Exploration of Africa* (New York: Harry N. Abrams, 1993), 19.

19. Romano Guardini, *The End of the Modern World* (Chicago: Henry Regenery, 1968), 51.

20. As James Baldwin points out:

So that, for example, when I talk about colonialism—which is also a word that can be defined—it refers to European domination of what we now call under-developed countries. It also refers to, no matter what the previous colonial powers may say, to the fact that these people entered those continents not to save them, not, no not, to bring the Cross of Christ or the Bible—though they did; that was a detail. And still less to inculcate into them a notion of political democracy. The truth is that they walked in and they stayed in, and recklessly destroyed whatever was in their way, in order to make money. And this is what we call the rise of capitalism, which is a pre-phase covering an eternity of crimes.

Nationalism, Colonialism, and the United States, a forum (pamphlet) sponsored by the Liberation Committee for Africa on its First Anniversary Celebration, June 2, 1961, 23–24.

21. Jean-François Lyotard, *Peregrinations* (New York: Columbia University Press, 1988), 18. The use that Lyotard makes of the term "pretext" is akin to what I have elsewhere labeled the stance of "false double negation." Tsenay Serequeberhan, *Our Heritage* (Lanham, MD: Rowman and Littlefield, 2000), 62.

22. Placide Tempels, *Bantu Philosophy* (Paris: Présence Africaine, 1969), 171–72.

23. Edward W. Said, *The Pen and the Sword: Conversations with David Barsamian* (Monroe, ME: Common Courage Press, 1994), 66.

24. Rudyard Kipling, "The White Man's Burden (1899)," in T. S. Eliot, *A Choice of Kipling's Verse* (New York: Anchor Books, 1962), 143–45.

25. Said, *The Pen and the Sword*, 68.

26. Cheikh H. Kane, *L'aventure ambiguë* (Paris: Julliard, 1961). This work of historical fiction is an excellent illustration of the castrating effects of this pedagogy.

27. For more on this, see my discussion of "Europeanized" and "non-Europeanized" in "African Philosophy: The Point in Question," in *African Philosophy*, 8–9.

28. In this regard, we read in a standard 1980s world history college textbook:

> The initial response of African and Asian rulers was to try to drive the . . . foreigners away. . . . Violent antiforeign [sic] reactions exploded . . . again and again, but the superior military technology of the . . . West almost invariably prevailed. Beaten in battle, many Africans and Asians concentrated on preserving their cultural traditions . . . Others found themselves forced to reconsider their initial hostility. Some (like Ismail of Egypt) concluded that the West was indeed superior in some ways and that it was necessary to reform their societies and copy European achievements.

John P. McKay, Bennett D. Hill, and John Buckler, *A History of Western Society*, 3rd ed. (Boston: Houghton Mifflin, 1987), 849. The reader ought to note how, in their detached and supposedly "objective" presentation, the authors of the above quoted textbook render a normalizing service to the brutal and abnormal eventuation of colonial conquest.

29. Basil Davidson, *Africa in Modern History* (New York: Penguin, 1985), 82–83.

30. Ibid., 43.

31. I borrow this formulation from Said, *The Pen and the Sword*, 67.

32. It is important to note that there is nothing pacific about "pacification"; it is the systematic destruction of any form of resistance imposed on an indigenous society by a colonizing power. It took the French circa forty years, from 1831 to 1870, to "pacify" Algeria. It is important to note that no form of villainy, barbarity, or cruelty is spared in such undertakings. And so, by "intellectual-cultural" pacification, I mean to indicate a similar kind of ideological eradication.

33. Frantz Fanon, *Les damnés de la terre* (Paris: François Maspero, 1974), 14; *The Wretched of the Earth*, trans. Constance Farrington (New York: Grove Press, 1968), 46.

34. As quoted by Marcien Towa in "Propositions sur l'identité culturelle," *Présence Africaine*, no. 109 (1979): 85.

35. Léopold Sédar Senghor, *On African Socialism*, trans. Mercer Cook (New York: Praeger, 1964), 82.

36. Julius K. Nyerere, "Africa: The Current Situation," *African Philosophy* 11, no. 1 (June 1998): 8.

37. Albert Memmi, *The Colonizer and the Colonized* (Boston: Beacon, 1965), 118.

38. Eliot, *A Choice of Kipling's Verse*, 143.

39. It should be clear that the designation "Dark Ages" is not a self-designation but a derogatory label imposed on the medieval past by a postmedieval assessment that sees itself as expressing the views of a progressively ascending enlightened age.

40. Chinua Achebe, *Home and Exile* (New York: Anchor Books, 2000), 26–27.

41. To this day, the images of Africa that one finds in comic books—such as Tarzan and Tintin—for example, along with the textbook renditions of African primitiveness and savagery, are not gratuitous. In the political economy of colonialism, and in the present context of Western hegemony, they are part of the "normal science" discourse, of everyday life, that in the guise of objective (or innocent or "funny," as in comics) descriptions construe the images of Africa that legitimated—and still legitimate—the pervasiveness and acceptance of Western dominance.

42. By "normal discourse"—analogously with Kuhn's "normal science" (see note 5 above)—I mean a discourse that presupposes an established paradigm—in this case, a paradigm of thought that takes for granted Western supremacy/hegemony. For example, in a recent interview, the

neoconservative ideologue Robert Kagan, in response to a question regarding the USA's invasion of Iraq, asks rhetorically: "And what are you going to do when the civilized come up against the primitive?" (*New York Times Magazine*, February 16, 2003, 11). This, then, is the "normal discourse" of a "thinking" that necessarily functions within the parameters of a paradigm of thought that takes for granted Western supremacy.

43. Edward W. Said, "The Politics of Knowledge," in *Reflections on Exile and Other Essays* (Cambridge, MA: Harvard University Press, 2000), 376.

44. On this subject, see my book *Contested Memory: The Icons of the Occidental Tradition* (Trenton, NJ: Africa World Press, 2007). See also chapter 6 of Serequeberhan, *Our Heritage*.

45. Gianni Vattimo, *La società trasparente* (Milan: Garzanti, 1989), 10.

46. For a detailed explication of what "double game" means, in this context, see chapter 1 of Serequeberhan, *Contested Memory*.

47. As Gerald Caplan puts it: "In 1960, a resolution at the United Nations General Assembly calling for the independence of all colonies was opposed by every European colonial power—Britain, France, Portugal, Belgium and Spain—plus the US and South Africa." Caplan, *The Betrayal of Africa* (Toronto: Groundwood Books, 2008), 34.

48. Frantz Fanon, "Vérités premiéres à propos du probléme colonial" in *Pour la revolution Africaine* (Paris: François Maspero, 1964), 141. This chapter was originally published, as an article, in *El Moudjahid*, no. 27 (July 22, 1958).

49. On this subject, see Martin Khor, "Colonialism Redux," 18–20, and Jerry Mander, "The Dark Side of Globalization," 9–14, both in *The Nation* 263, no. 3 (July 15/22, 1996); and Serge Latouche, *The Westernization of the World* (Cambridge: Polity Press, 1996). I say "under various guises and new modalities" because, as Lewis R. Gordon has noted: "There was a time in which the colony was a legitimate endeavor. Today, colonies are constructed in the face of their denial. It is morally and politically embarrassing to own and to found 'colonies,' so the same institutions are created without being *named as such.*" *Disciplinary Decadence* (Boulder, CO: Paradigm, 2006), 140n28.

In this regard, it ought to be noted that, "according to a U.S. Senate Foreign relations Committee report," the USA is presently building in Baghdad, Iraq, an embassy "the size of Vatican City," which has its own "defense force" and comprises "21 buildings on 104 acres." "New U.S. Embassy in Iraq Cloaked in Mystery," Associated Press, April 14, 2006, http://www.msnbc.msn.com/id/12319798/. Will Iraq's sovereignty survive the weight of all this cement? It is in this manner that "colonies are constructed in the face of their denial." On this point, see also Walter Pincus's article "U.S. Africa Command Brings New Concerns," *Washing-*

ton Post, May 28, 2007, A13, http://www.washingtonpost.com/wp-dyn/content/article/2007/05/27/AR2007052700978.html.

50. Sembène Ousmane, *Xala* (Chicago: Lawrence Hill, 1976), 84, emphasis added.

51. Writing as far back as 1957, for example, Albert Memmi tells us: "Today, the economic motives of colonial undertakings are revealed by every historian of colonialism. The cultural and moral mission of a colonizer, even in the beginning, is no longer tenable" (*The Colonizer and the Colonized*, 3). Or as the Canadian philosopher Charles Taylor points out: "The days are long gone when Europeans and other Westerners could consider their experience and culture as the norm toward which the whole of humanity was headed, so that the other could be understood as an earlier stage on the same road that they had trodden." Taylor, "Understanding the Other: A Gadamerian View on Conceptual Schemes," in *Gadamer's Century*, ed. Jeff Malpas, Ulrich Arnswald, and Jens Kertscher (Cambridge, MA: MIT Press, 2002), 279.

52. Hans-Georg Gadamer, *The Enigma of Health* (Stanford, CA: Stanford University Press, 1996), 139.

53. Tsenay Serequeberhan, "The Critique of Eurocentrism and the Practice of African Philosophy," in *Postcolonial African Philosophy*, ed. Emmanuel Chukwudi Eze (Cambridge, MA: Blackwell, 1997), 142.

54. Cornelius Castoriadis, *Philosophy, Politics, Autonomy*, ed. David A. Curtis (New York: Oxford University Press, 1991), 200–201. In full: "Factually speaking, the West has been and remains victorious—and not only through the force of its weapons: it remains so through its ideas, through its 'models' of growth and development, through the statist and other structures which, having been created by it, are today adopted everywhere."

55. Achebe, *Home and Exile*, 27. As Chinua Achebe points out regarding Nigeria:

The fear that should nightly haunt our leaders (but does not) is that they may already have betrayed irretrievably Nigeria's high destiny. The countless billions that a generous Providence poured into our national coffers in the last ten years (1972–1982) would have been enough to launch this nation into the middle-rank of developed nations and transformed the lives of our poor and needy. But what have we done with it? Stolen and salted away by people in power and their accomplices. Squandered in uncontrolled importation of all kinds of useless consumer merchandise . . . Embezzled through inflated contracts to an increasing army of party loyalists . . . Consumed in the escalating salaries of a grossly overstaffed and unproductive public service. And so on ad infinitum.

Achebe, *The Trouble with Nigeria* (Enugu, Nigeria: Fourth Dimension, 1983), 2–3. One need not subscribe to Achebe's theological scaffolding to recognize that *mutatis mutandis*, what he says about Nigeria is equally applicable to most of the continent.

56. Martin Plaut, "The UN's All-Pervasive Role in Africa," *BBC News*, July 18, 2007, http://news.bbc.co.uk/go/pr/fr/-/1/hi/world/africa/6903196.stm.

57. As Kwame Nkrumah noted long ago: "Although apparently strong because of their support from neocolonialists and imperialists, they are extremely vulnerable. Their survival depends on foreign support. Once this vital link is broken, they become powerless to maintain their positions and privileges." *Class Struggle in Africa* (New York: International, 1975), 12.

A case in point is Mengistu Hailemariam's Ethiopia that had to switch patrons, from the USA to the USSR, as a result of President Carter's "human rights"–oriented foreign policy. When the Carter administration made it difficult for Mengistu to secure arms in order to squash domestic opposition and, more urgently, to prosecute the colonial war in Eritrea, he became, overnight, a Marxist-Leninist and realigned Ethiopia with the USSR, in the then raging cold war; soon thereafter, with the demise of the USSR, lacking a foreign prop to protect it from the Eritrean anti-colonial struggle, Mengistu's military dictatorship ("a house of cards") collapsed.

58. Elizabeth Blunt, "Corruption 'Costs Africa billions,'" *BBC News*, September 18, 2002, http://news.bbc.co.uk/2/hi/africa/2265387.stm.

59. Fanon, *Les damnés de la terre*, 94.

60. On this point, see chapter 4 of Gerald Caplan's *The Betrayal of Africa*.

61. Said, *Reflections on Exile*, 379.

62. Fanon, *Les damnés de la terre*, 117; *Wretched of the Earth*, 176. For a recent discussion of the enduring relevance of Fanon, for thinking the political situation of contemporary African, see Lewis R. Gordon's *An Introduction to Africana Philosophy* (New York: Cambridge University Press, 2008), 220–48.

63. On this point, see Robert Bernasconi, "Can Development Theory Break with Its Past? Endogenous Development in Africa and the Old Imperialism," *African Philosophy* 11, no. 1 (June 1998): 23–34.

64. Amílcar Cabral, *Return to the Source: Selected Speeches* (New York: Monthly Review Press, 1973), 52.

65. Herbert Marcuse, "The Individual in the Great Society," in *The Essential Marcuse*, ed. Andrew Feenberg and William Leiss (Boston: Beacon, 2007), 10. As if confirming the above observation, Henry Kissinger, in a 1970 memo on Allende to Richard Nixon, states: "The example of

a successful elected Marxist government in Chile would surely have an impact—and even precedent value for—other parts of the world. . . . The imitative spread of similar phenomena elsewhere would in turn significantly affect the world balance and our position in it." As quoted by Naomi Klein in "Latin America's Shock Resistance," *The Nation* 285, no. 17 (November 2007): 28.

Beyond Gendercentric Models

Restoring Motherhood to Yoruba Discourses of Art and Aesthetics

Oyèrónké̩ Oyěwùmí

Gendercentric models are rife in African Studies, and African art historical studies are no exception. Approaches that assume a gender-dichotomized view of society are necessarily male-dominant, because in our time, patriarchy is the main expression of gender divisions. Two claims emerge from this biased branding of African art. First, that traditionally in Africa only men make art or engage in the production of important art. Second, that materials for making art are gender-specific: metals are for men, clay is for women; so goes the refrain. In fact, the second claim is actually expressed as a restriction against women's use of iron, and there is no obverse understanding that men are or can be constrained from using any material, including clay. Being male is assumed to be, everywhere in "traditional Africa," a mark of privilege, if not license. The effect of this antifemale stance is to place women at the receiving end of the gaze.

But how and where did the claims that women are not artists, and that materials for making art are gender identifiable, originate? Many of these genderist and sexist ideas are based on observations of white adventurers, colonial ethnographers, missionaries, and colonial officials whose ethnocentric biases are very much tied up with their dominant positions and ideas about white racial and cultural superiority. Much of their intellectual engagement with Africa has been about how to fit African lives into their prefabricated theories. Despite the fact that some of the most reprehensible early European racist ideas about Africans have been thoroughly discredited, sexist notions have not. But this is not to say that racism and sexism are not intertwined.

Why, then, do the most egregious gender-discriminatory claims continue to gain traction? Three main reasons are immediately apparent. First, many of the assumptions that white cultural imperialists and colonizers made about African art and societies have been left largely unquestioned. Embraced as received scholarly ideas, such claims are repeated across time and space by contemporary writers of all stripes, including Africans. Second, I suspect that some African male scholars have also embraced such sexist statements because they erroneously believe that to do so favors them today as a gender-identified group. Finally, many scholars continue to treat gender categories and gender dichotomies as natural, and therefore take expressions and practices of male dominance for granted in any time or place in which they are found. Decades of research have shown that gender is historical and socially constructed. I make a distinction between what I call genderist claims and sexist claims. Genderism is the idea that gender categories in human organization are timeless and universal. Sexism is the idea that male dominance is natural.

More important, the homogenization and consequent miniaturizing of Africa's many nations, peoples, and cultures are the first indications of the problem of overly broad generalizations. Such universalizing about the continent is difficult to sustain, if not totally irrational. With regard to art and artistry in particular, this kind of continent-wide generalization is simply meaningless. Fundamentally, the most egregious part of the problem is the way in which such sweeping statements place the whole of the continent under the Western gaze, arrogantly reducing such a huge, diverse entity into one place and a single unit of analysis. As soon as one attempts to apply those statements to particular cultures and specific places, however, one discovers that such claims are false, or at best wanting. For example, in a paper on "African" ceramics, Jerome Vogel writes: "Throughout Africa, pottery is made primarily by women. . . . Men do make pots among a few groups, like the Hausa of Northern Nigeria, but this is an exception."[1]

The idea that millions of Hausa men and women are among "a few groups" is laughable, and begs the question: Who made the rules from which millions of Hausa are an exception? Certainly not Hausa people. From the perspective of Hausa communities in which men make pots, there is nothing exceptional about it, because there is no such rule. It is just a fact, not an exception. The exception exists only in the glazed eyes of the Western beholder. We have since discovered more "exceptions" across the continent to this Euro-American–made rule that African men do not make pottery; in Ghana, Angola, Democratic Republic of Congo, and Zambia, we find men sculpting clay in a variety of ethnic groups and nationalities.[2]

In the face of these biases, distortions, misrepresentations, and misunderstandings, it is clear that we must develop and highlight Africa-centered approaches. Over the years, a number of African scholars have advocated for indigenous paradigms in apprehending art and artistry, and here are two examples. The cultural studies scholar Olabiyi Yai admonishes us that in approaching African art, we must examine all taken-for-granted assumptions, even if they are foundational to our disciplines, and that we must take indigenous discourses on art and art history seriously in our discussions.[3] Similarly, art historian Rowland Abiodun advises that in the study of African art, we must try to understand an artwork in its cultural depth, as the expression of local thought or belief systems.[4]

Taking seriously the cautionary advice of both Yai and Abiodun, my goal in this chapter is to interrogate prevailing gendered approaches to traditional Yoruba art and art history, and then, drawing from Yoruba cultural values and social practices, elaborate the relationship between art and motherhood, procreation and artistry. In *The Invention of Women,* I show that gender is not an ontological category in the Yoruba world. In contrast, in Western thought gender is assumed to be ontological, and therefore timeless and universal. Consequently, the institution of motherhood in Western and scholarly discourses that derive from their dominance is represented as paradigmatic of female gender. But in the Yoruba ethos, motherhood is not about gender.

The presence of categories that have to do with procreation and motherhood does not necessarily suggest the inherent nature of gender categories. In fact, as I argued in an earlier work, gender in Yoruba society is a colonial category that emerged during the period of European ascendancy and dominance. Gender by definition is a duality: it is about two categories in relation to each other, often oppositionally constructed. Motherhood in the Yoruba worldsense is a singular category that is unparalleled by any other. Fatherhood is not its counterpart. The roots of gender categories in contemporary Yoruba society are colonial.

Gender and Yoruba Art

Globally, Yoruba art is one of the most recognized and celebrated African arts. It is seen as one of the most important in representing the antiquity, mastery, and depth of knowledge on the continent. Consequently, there is no better place to interrogate some of the most pressing issues in African art historical studies than in this setting. In Yoruba art studies, we see a different facet of the problem of gendering and sexism in interpretation of African art. What we find here is a conundrum. In the early twentieth century, a collection of lifelike terra-cotta and brass sculptures were excavated in and around Ile-Ife, the Yoruba ancestral home. These sculptures are regarded as exquisite pieces of "high" art bearing the mark of civilization.

Because many of the sculptures are made of clay (terra-cotta), it became a problem for those interpreters of African art who use the gendered model of "women use clay, and men use metals." Because Western art distinguishes between male art and women's craft, expressing an antifemale stance, pottery making in Africa as in Europe has been reduced to a "domestic" craft, thus rendering difficult any acknowledgment of female authorship of great art. What, then, are Western scholars to make of Ife terra-cotta sculptures, which are regarded as fine art but made of clay in a society in which these scholars have a priori declared that "clay is for girls, and metals are for boys"?

Let us consider these questions. For five decades after the excavation of the Ife sculptures, no question was raised about the gender identity of the ancient artists because it was assumed that men had made the pieces. Art historian Henry Drewal finally posed the question. In his paper "Ife: Origins of Art and Civilization," he asked, "Were the creators of these exquisite works women or men?"[5] His immediate answer is puzzling enough, given that the sculptures date back to the eleventh century. Drewal writes, "An analysis of the sculpting technique used in the terracotta suggested that the artists were male."[6] What analysis? Whose analysis? What technique? No, Drewal did not do the "gender test" on these terra-cottas himself; he attributes the gendered analysis to Frank Willett, an archaeologist, in a footnote. On consulting the authoritative Willett text, we discover that his "analysis" is based on mere conjecture. According to Willett, because the internal surface of the terra-cotta sculpture is rough and unfinished, it is distinguishable from women's domestic pottery, which is invariably smoothed inside and out. Therefore, he concludes, the terra-cottas could not have been made by women.[7]

Two questions come to mind: How do we know that Yoruba pottery is made by women and only women? And how do smoothness and roughness of the surface become a measure of the gender identity of artists? Drewal correctly surmised that the finish of the pieces couldn't tell us about the sex of the artists, "only that pots and sculptures serve different functions." Even then, one of the sculptures represented an exception to the Willett-made rule that Yoruba pots have smooth exteriors but the terra-cotta have rough exteriors. At least one of the terra-cotta heads "has such a smooth interior."[8] Based on this observation, Drewal finally dispenses with Willett's claim that the sculptures had been made by men and only men. He writes that because the Yoruba tradition that women, not men, work the clay is deeply rooted, he could not discount the possibility that female artists made the Ife heads. Given that the Yoruba world was not gendered or dichotomized into male and female, we have to question Drewal's bold claim that the Yoruba have such a gendered tradition. Neither Drewal nor any other scholar has accounted for such gender claims about Yoruba art. For Drewal, as a logical outgrowth of his gender model, evidence of Yoruba women's hands in the Ife terra-cotta could not be ignored.

However, Drewal did not stop there. Given the grandness of these works of art, he could not leave the men out as their cocreators. Despite his earlier assertions about Yoruba women's monopoly of clay art, he could not grant women the sole authorship of these exquisite sculptures. He concluded therefore that "artistic efforts done by both men and women cannot be ruled out in the case of Ife art,"[9] thus bringing resolution to the European-created gender question of the anatomic identity of the ancient Ife artist, a question that does not derive from Yoruba art, values, or social practices.

In her paper titled "Art, History, and Gender: Women and Clay in West Africa," Marla Berns questions male dominance in the interpretation of African art, and challenges the refusal of scholars to grant women authorship of figural sculptures, including the Ife pieces. She points out that even the description of such figural clay sculptures as terra-cotta to distinguish them from pottery maintains the hierarchy that the former is art and is of a higher order than the latter, which are said to be made by women.[10] Berns then goes on to commend Drewal for breaching the tradition of male-dominant interpretations when he recognized Yoruba women's role in cocreating the Ife sculptures.

However, while I would note Drewal's recognition of Yoruba women's role in the production of Ife art, I question any suggestion that his interpretation is less male-biased or problematic. For one thing, he insists that men shared the making of the clay sculptures with women, but neither he nor other art historians would subject the corresponding metal sculptures to any gender tests; it was clear to them that the brass heads, which were found in the same archaeological dig, were made by men, and men alone. But how do they know this?

Both Berns and I are concerned about male dominance in the interpretation of African art, which has resulted in denying women mastery and authorship of important works, while at the same time downgrading their artistic production to the level of craft.[11] However, Berns does not question the gender-dichotomized interpretation of African art. If anything, she states categorically that "there is little doubt that sexual difference accounts for who makes what kinds of art in Africa."[12] This statement is baseless, and is no different from Willett's claim that because "domestic pottery in the whole of Africa is normally made by women of the community, the terracotta sculptures are likely to have been made by men at Ife."[13] We have already mentioned the millions of exceptions to this claim that have been found all over the continent.

More specifically, I am concerned about not only sexism, but also genderism—the idea that gender categories are operational in the organization, production, and appreciation of Yoruba art. In traditional Yoruba society, there is no universal category for females that you can label "women of the community." Females who are born into a lineage (sisters) belong to a category different from and superior to that of females married into the same lineage (wives), and the interests of these two female groupings are often different, and are sometimes opposed. Females born into the lineage are grouped together with their male counterparts (brothers) as *omo ile* and their interests are presented as one and the same, in contrast to that of *iyawo ile* (wives married to the males of the lineage).

We see *iyawo ile* artists in action in art historian Bolaji Campbell's account of shrine paintings in Yorubaland. In the book *Painting for the Gods: Art and Aesthetics of Yoruba Religious Murals*, he documents and analyzes shrine paintings in different Yoruba towns. In his discussion of Oluorogbo-lineage shrine paintings in Ile ife, Campbell writes: "The iyawo'le, that is, the women married into the household who are mandated to paint the shrine walls, begin the arduous task of the procurement and preparation of the necessary materials for the paintings."[14] He further points out that "women married into the Oluorogbo lineage are very enthusiastic about participating. . . . It is believed that the divinity would accede to most of their manifold requests, including money, health, and the gift of children."[15]

The genderism and sexism of Africanist art historians, feminist and nonfeminist alike, are certainly an issue. The more fundamental problem, however, is their ethnocentrism, which allows them to make such arrogant and gratuitous statements, reduce Africa to one place, one unit of analysis, in the face of evidence that many societies do not fit their theories, and that many more societies have been branded though unstudied. In essence, they are dismissive of African categories and understanding of their own cultures. The gendered paradigm is inseparable from their Eurocentrism. Such a model has made it extremely difficult to study Africa, African art, art history, and aesthetics in all their continental variety and the multivarious local models that may or may not have to do with gender. With regard to Yoruba visual arts, it is interesting to note that two generations of art historians have underscored the idea that "Yoruba culture has its own built-in internal mechanisms and theories of critical evaluation."[16] Regrettably, however, many of them do not seem to understand that gender dichotomies are not inherent in any art form; rather, gender models are part of the critical apparatus that they have inherited from the European and American intellectual tradition, and they must be recognized as such.

What do Yoruba history and culture tell us about the provenance of art and artistry, eschewing the unfounded gendered Western impositions on a people and their aesthetics and cultural products? The twisting and turning of Drewal and Willett that we see in their attempts at establishing the gender of Ife classical artists is a function not of the art in and of itself, or of Yoruba social practices; rather, it is due to the erroneous assumption that in ancient Yoruba society artistry was organized around the male and female anatomy. This could not be further from the truth. In Yoruba towns, specialized occupations like pot making, smithing, and the like are inhered in particular lineage groups, not individuals as men or women. Within such lineage guilds, male and female members are free to participate, as they will, and according to mode of entry into the family, birth or marriage, as we noted with the shrine paintings.

As I pointed out earlier, in the European-derived art historical literature, clay and metals draw the lines of distinction between female craft and male art, respectively. But this was not the line of distinction in Yoruba society. For example, some of the Ife naturalistic sculptures were made of brass and some were made of clay, though all of them seem to have been from the same time and place. Brass is associated with the Osun, a female deity. In Yoruba stories of creation, the god Obatala, the creator divinity, is represented as male in some Yoruba localities and female in others. She or he is said to make humans with clay and then use Ogun's implements (iron) to delineate and refine their features. Ogun is a male divinity. The fact that Obatala is depicted as male in some communities and female in other Yoruba localities suggests that his or her gender identity is not important to the role attributed to the creator god. In my earlier work, I have shown that anatomic distinctions in Yoruba culture are incidental and do not define social hierarchy, occupations, or functions.[17] The point is that in Yoruba social organization and practices, clay and metal are not opposed at any level.

Studies of Yoruba metal sculpture bear this out. In art historian C. O Adepegba's detailed study of Yoruba metal sculptures, we learn the following facts:

1. The most common metal in old Yoruba sculpture is brass, which is an alloy.
2. Copper, lead, and iron are some of the other metals used.
3. Some metals are associated with certain orisha and their votaries: Ogun (iron), Obatala (Oje/lead), Osun (brass/ide).
4. Yoruba smiths are known as *agbede*, but jewelsmiths who work on nonferrous metals are distinguished from blacksmiths.

Adepegba continues: "[Smiths] are, however, more popularly known by their lineage names: *Asude* in Ibadan and Ilorin, *Esude* in Edomowo and *Isude* in Ogbomoso. In Idomowo as well as in Obo Ayegunle, brasscasting was more or less a community profession. The entire people of Idomowo are known as *Esude ma gbowo oya, egbowo ide*."[18]

This lineage-based specialization is very much in line with my analysis in an earlier study,[19] where I argued that specialized professions and crafts were the prerogative of specific lineages in the polity. The division of labor here was lineage-based in that lineage membership, not the anatomy, was required to practice such professions. In research that Adepegba conducted in the 1970s across Yorubaland, he documents the disappearance of most of the centers of brasscasting and points out some of the changes that were well under way where the art form was still present. Because these findings are important for understanding Yoruba traditions and the rapid social change in these traditions that was taking place, I will quote him at some length:

> For example in Idomowo, the only traces of the survivors of the old brasscasters are a few goldsmiths who find their new craft very close to the family occupation and more rewarding. In Obo Ayegunle, only two of the brasscasters who worked in the town in the early 1970's remain. The situation in Ogbomoso is almost the same. In fact the only artisan who is still actively engaged in figure casting learned the craft from the Isude. In Ibadan, the remaining women who sell products of brasscasters display their goods as a kind of family glory.[20]

One cannot overemphasize the need to pay attention to history and social change and the vacuums that are created and are often filled with the gender-prejudice of our newfangled postcolonial world. Fortunately, the male bias in the documentation and analysis of Yoruba art and art history has not passed unremarked. Art historian Rowland Abiodun made the point that even though "much of Yoruba religious activity and aesthetic concerns appear to be male-dominated, we have not much authority from Yoruba oral traditions and visual art for assuming that this picture is accurate."[21]

Abiodun's perceptive comment notwithstanding, he, too, partakes of gender exclusion. For example, in a volume he coedited titled *The Yoruba Artist*, only one chapter recognizes the artistry of Yoruba females, and it characterizes them as verbal and not visual artists. No doubt verbal artistry is highly valued in Yoruba society, as it should be, but this does not mean that the full range of female artistry goes unrecognized. Another dimension of the inherited Eurocentric gender model is apparent in the work of other Yoruba art historians, Babatunde Lawal and Bolaji Campbell, who are quick to embrace Obatala (the creator god who molded humans) as a male divinity, discounting the traditions that identify the god as female. Although Campbell acknowledges that Obatala is recognized as female in some Yoruba communities, he chooses to represent the deity as

male because one Ifa "divination text does not suggest that Obatala
was a female divinity."[22] Here we get a glimpse of the kind of choices
scholars make that result in the manufacture of gender models for
the Yoruba where such notions are alien. Campbell acknowledges
the possibility of a move toward patriarchy when he writes that the
shift in gender of the orisha Obatala may be due to males' sudden
rise to prominence during the colonial period. Regrettably, he does
not incorporate this insight into the larger body of his study of orisha shrine paintings and ultimately reproduces the Eurocentric patriarchal model.[23]

The Art of Motherhood

Representations of motherhood in Yoruba culture have artistic dimensions. Consequently, in this section I want to consider the link-
ages between art and motherhood, and the larger meaning of motherhood in the traditions. But before I get to Yoruba constructions of
motherhood, inescapably, we have to note that in the gendercentric
European models that have dominated interpretations of Yoruba art,
motherhood is paradigmatic of gender.

Though female reproduction is a human universal, the meanings
attached to motherhood are diverse across cultures. Western accounts
of motherhood reduce it to a gender category: mother is represented
as a woman first and foremost, a category that is perceived to be customarily disadvantaged and oppressed, because women are subordinate to males, who are the privileged group. The traditional Yoruba
elaboration of motherhood is radically different, and is anything but
gendered. The complexity of the Yoruba portrayal of motherhood
will emerge shortly in an examination of art and artistry.

Art historian Babatunde Lawal comments on the connection between art and motherhood:

> Yoruba identify a work of art as ona, that is, an embodiment
> of creative skills, implicating the archetypal action of Obat-
> ala, the creativity deity and patron of the Yoruba artist. The
> process of creating a work of art is called onayiya, a term
> implicated in [a]prayer for an expectant mother. "Ki orisa
> ya ona re koni." (May the orisha fashion for us a good work
> of art.)[24]

He continues, explaining, "The fact that the female body mediates Obtala's creation has led some to translate *iya*, the Yoruba word for mother, as 'someone from whom another life is fashioned' or the body 'from which we are created.'"[25] Indeed, *Iya* is the term for "mother" in the Yoruba language, and it implicates the verb *ya*, which is to draw, to carve, or to fashion. For Yai, another scholar, the concept is best captured in expressions such as: "ya ere (to carve), ya aworan (to design or paint)."[26] Lawal, however, gives an unduly passive interpretation by portraying the role of mothers in procreation as if they are bystanders (vessels) rather than cocreators of the child with the deity Obatala. The greeting to an expectant mother (May the orisha fashion for us a good work of art) not only refers to Obatala (the creator deity), but is also directed at the *ori* (inner head, fate) of the hopeful mother. The greeting is an invocation to the ori of the expectant mother to support and bless her through the arduous process of birthing a child.

Ori in Yoruba spirituality is a deity in its own right. Symbolized by the physical head, it is recognized as the seat of fate for each human being, and the original source of one's destiny. As Ifa divination texts tell us, there is nothing that happens to a particular human being that is not supported by his or her ori. In moments of danger, the first God to be invoked is one's ori, followed by an appeal to the ori of one's mother. "Ori'yami" (my mother's ori) is the ultimate cry of alarm, warning, and sorrow in Yoruba society, uttered by anyone in distress. In the culture at large and more specifically for expectant mothers, there is no moment of greater danger than the birthing of a child. Hence, pregnancy is a period during which the ori is constantly invoked by family members and well-wishers alike. The first and subsequently constant greeting to the new mother and her family members is "Eku ewu omo" (Greetings for surviving the dangers of childbirth).

Consider this description of the traditional birthing process:

> When the expectant mother is in labor, the parent (grand-mother) will gather scraps of cloth or other disused clothing nearby and she will be provided with a piece of abiwere soap [formulated to facilitate the birthing process] that had been prepared beforehand. She will proceed to take a bath. Afterwards, she will return to the room, kneeling on a mat in what is the [Yoruba] cultural birthing posture. [Meanwhile], her restive mother will be pacing up and down, going in and

out of the house. But hardly would other residents of the compound know what is going on. Still, given the mother's strange demeanor, it is almost impossible for the neighbors not to suspect that something is amiss. She remains restless but her neighbors will pretend not to notice. Once in a while, she will check on her daughter in the room, invoking her ori, entreating orisa, that the Owner of the Heavens will pull them through.[27]

In the Yoruba cosmology, the moment of preearthly creation (of individual humans)—*akunleyan*—and the moment of procreation—*ikunle abiyamo*—are regarded as one and the same. Though the two moments are separated temporally, they are visually represented by ikunle abiyamo, a pose that is prevalent in Yoruba art. Accordingly, ikunle abiyamo refers to the kneeling of a mother in labor. Abiodun explains that the kneeling nude woman figure symbolizes humanity choosing its destiny in heaven (otherworld).[28] I could not agree more. In this sense, mothers are representative of humanity, ungendered. In this Yoruba conception, there is no male-as-norm of the Western gendercentric model, in which only men can represent universal human attributes.

It is obvious that there is a huge gap between the Eurocentric worldview that is used to interpret Yoruba images and the Yoruba depiction of their own art. When the kneeling sculpture of a Yoruba woman is viewed through a Eurocentric male-dominant lens, the image they see is one of a woman (wife, inferior, subordinated creature) kneeling down, a pose that is viewed as one of subjection. For the Yoruba and the traditional artists who created those images, however, the image represents a spiritual pose assumed by a mother, a powerful human being, kneeling in front of the Supreme Being, representing each and every member of the human race: her children. Here motherhood is an inclusive category; mothers have male and female children and therefore are universal representatives of the human.

Centering Yoruba experiences of motherhood reveals that motherhood is not merely an earthly institution: it is otherworldly, preearthly, pregestational, presocial, prenatal, postnatal, and lifelong. Thus relationship between a mother and a child then is timeless. The previously mentioned process of pre-earthly creation—*akunleyan*—the moment of choosing one's fate in the otherworld before each human makes that journey to the world—is, quintessentially, a ritual of choosing one's mother. The connectedness of motherhood and aesthetics continues through the physical birthing process and postpartum care of the infant. All these processes are regarded as *onayiya*—making art—among other things. Postpartum care of the infant in the first months of life requires continuous molding (analogous to the molding of clay) of the head into a beautiful shape. But of course, the most aesthetically pleasing sight is the child, in and of itself.

We see another linkage of aesthetics and motherhood in Abiodun's description of the epa masks of northeastern Yorubaland:

> In the helmet masks of north-eastern Yoruba (sometimes known generically as elefon or epa) a common theme in the superstructure is the kneeling of a woman with two children, sometimes called Otonporo, the pride of elefon. During a festival at Ikerin, it is singled out for praise she is an embodiment of all that can be considered beautiful in Yoruba context. Beauty in this context includes the gift of children, which most women pray for during the festival. Otonporo is painted with black, red, yellow and white colors to make her beauty visible even at a distance.[29]

Children are emblematic of beauty in Yoruba representations, and as earthly cocreators of these beauties, mothers have a unique role to play in the lives of their children, and hence the community. The vagina is also called *Iyamapo*, a name that arises from its creative role in making and molding babies as works of art. In the orisha pantheon of divinities, there is one named Iyamapo. Her roles as mother and artist are wonderfully linked. We see this in the yearly festival of Iyamapo, a rock-dwelling deity in Igbetti. At the festival, the worshippers sing a song of prayer to the Great Mother that she might never lose the tie (oja) that fastens her children, the townspeople, securely on her back. Iyamapo is regarded as the tutelary deity of artists, particularly of potters and dyers.[30]

Art as Visual *Oriki*

Thus far, we have been considering Yoruba elaboration of the aesthetic functions of motherhood, and the role of mothers in the crea-

tion of living art, also known as children. But the culture also recognizes their role in the production of both visual and verbal art. I
contend that the dominance of females in the making of *oriki* (praise
poetry) and shrine paintings stems from their unique role as mothers. In reality, the impetus for visual and verbal arts is one and the
same: these beautiful creations represent adornments for the gods and
herald the celebration of their greatest gift to humans—children. Because mothers are central to the process of creation and procreation,
it is not surprising that their artistry often flows from it. Because each
and every one of us is born of a mother, no one male or female is excluded from participating or enjoying the inheritance of the mother,
including her artistry.

Cultural studies scholar Olabiyi Yai proposes: "When approaching Yoruba art, an intellectual orientation that would be more
consonant with Yoruba traditions of scholarship would be to consider each individual Yoruba art work, and the entire corpus as
oriki (praise poetry). . . . Oriki is an unfinished and generative art
enterprise."[31]

Because mothers are central in the everyday production and reproduction of both children (as living art) and oriki, Yai's concept
of visual oriki is wonderfully brought to life (pun intended) by children, who are as the visual oriki rendered by their mothers. In everyday Yoruba life, mothers continuously verbally adorn their art,
and their ministrations intensify at certain times in the lives of their
children, such as when a daughter is giving birth. Giving birth is
one of those difficult times. Reciting a person's oriki has the effect
of arousing one to action so that one can put forth an excellent performance.

Mothers use oriki to praise, to build up, to adorn their children
and raise their self-esteem. Similarly, in the realm of religion, mothers as *iyawo'le* are charged with the annual painting of orisha shrines,
an undertaking that they describe as performing *ewa orisa*, a process
of imbuing, beautifying, and investing the sacred spaces of the orisha
with honor.[32] Images painted on wall shrines are, in the words of one
artist, *aso orisa*—clothing for the orisha, adornment for the gods.[33]
According to Campbell, These rituals of periodic renewal and painting serve as a bond that unites members of a particular lineage.[34] Who
better to enact these rituals of lineage renewal than mothers, who are
the reproducers of the lineage?

Conclusion: Anonymous Is Mother

The idea that the authorship of a particular artwork is difficult to establish is a major theme in African art studies. Hence the claim that historically, African artists have been anonymous. But anonymous to whom? They were certainly not nameless to their mothers, patrons, or communities. The lack of individual identification of traditional African artists has correctly been attributed to racial and cultural prejudice of the early European ethnographers, who rarely asked the question "Who made this" work of art?[35] Equally important is the fact that establishing individual authorship of art is very much tied up with its commodification and the pecuniary interests of Euro-American collectors.

My interest in this chapter has been to expose motherhood as yet another avenue, a route to making all forms of art. Motherhood should not be understood as a collective blanket of anonymity. Rather, there is no more individual relationship than that between a mother and each child; a bond that has motivated mother artists to engage in different kinds of visual and verbal arts. As documented, we see that in some cases, the process has been institutionalized in women's roles as mothers of the lineage.

The irony is that even though the African artist was said to wear a mask of anonymity, everyone could tell he was male, albeit a nameless male. Because of this male bias in the establishment of the provenance of traditional African art, it is clear that "anonymous" was female. In that vein, then, the role of mother as artist was anonymous, and so were mother artists. Consequently, we can say that "anonymous" is mother. But today she has a name because she is decolonized.

Notes

1. Jerome Vogel, "African Ceramics," in *Material Differences: Art and Identity in Africa*, ed. Frank Herreman (New York: Museum of African Art, 2003).

2. Marla C. Berns, "Art, History, and Gender: Women and Clay in West Africa," *African Archaeological Review* 11 (1993): 141.

3. Olabiyi Yai, "In Praise of Metonymy: The Concepts of 'Tradition' and 'Creativity' in the Transmission of Yoruba Artistry Over Time and Space," in *The Yoruba Artist: New Theoretical Perspectives on African Arts*,

ed. Rowland Abiodun, Henry J. Drewal, and John Pemberton (Washington: Smithsonian Institution Press, 1994), 107.

4. Abiodun, Drewal, and Pemberton, *The Yoruba Artist.*

5. Henry J. Drewal, "Ife: Origins of Art and Civilization," in *Nine Centuries of Yoruba Art,* ed. Henry J. Drewal, Rowland Abiodun, and Allen Wardwell (New York: Center for African Art, 1989), 71.

6. Ibid.

7. Frank Willett, *Ife in the History of West African Sculpture* (New York: McGraw Hill, 1967), 77.

8. Drewal, "Ife," 71.

9. Ibid.

10. Berns, "Art, History and Gender," 134.

11. Ibid.

12. Ibid., 130.

13. Willett, *Ife in the History of West African Sculpture,* 77.

14. Bolaji Campbell, *Painting for the Gods: Art and Aesthetics of Yoruba Religious Murals* (Trenton, NJ: Africa World Press, 2008), 80.

15. Ibid., 84.

16. Ibid., 14.

17. Oyèrónkéé Oyĕwùmí, *The Invention of Women: Making an African Sense of Western Gender Discourses* (Minneapolis: University of Minnesota Press, 1997).

18. Cornelius O. Adepegba, *Yoruba Metal Sculpture* (Ibadan: Ibadan University Press, 1991), 20.

19. Oyĕwùmí, *The Invention of Women.*

20. Adepegba, *Yoruba Metal Sculpture,* 20.

21. Rowland Abiodun, "Woman in Yoruba Religious Images," *African Languages and Cultures* 2, no. 1 (1989): 2.

22. Campbell, *Painting for the Gods,* 125.

23. Ibid., 124–25.

24. Babatunde Lawal, "Aworan: Representing the Self and Its Metaphysical Other in Yoruba Art," *Art Bulletin* 83, no. 3 (2001).

25. Ibid., 500.

26. Yai, "In Praise of Metonymy," 113.

27. Afolabi Olabimtan, ed., *Akojopo Iwadii Ijinle Asa Yoruba* (Ibadan, Nigeria: Macmillan, 1986), 139.

28. Abiodun, "Woman in Yoruba Religious Images," 12.

29. Ibid., 14.

30. J. A. Westcott and Peter Morton-Williams, "The Festival of Iyamapo," *Nigeria Magazine* 58 (1958): 212–24.

31. Yai, "In Praise of Metonymy," 107.

32. Campbell, *Painting for the Gods*, 101.

33. Ibid., 120.

34. Ibid.

35. Roslyn A. Walker, "Anonymous Has a Name: The Olowe of Ise," in Abiodun, Drewal, and Pemberton, *The Yoruba Artist*, 91.

Contributors

Lesley Cowling is a senior lecturer in journalism and media studies at Wits University, as well as an honorary research fellow in the Public Life of Ideas Network.

Marlene De La Cruz-Guzmán is a doctoral candidate in African literature in the Department of English at Ohio University. Her primary research areas are women's literature, critical theory, and African and diasporic literatures. She has received national and university fellowships, and has published articles on Sefi Atta, Laila Lalami, Yvonne Vera, Chimamanda Adichie, Chin Ce, and Zee Edgell, among others. She also serves as an editorial reviewer for the *Journal of African Literature and Culture*, and served as the chair of the African Literature Association Graduate Student Caucus. Originally from Guatemala, she has lived and conducted research in Belize, Morocco, Zimbabwe, and South Africa.

Carolyn Hamilton is NRF chair of Archive and Public Culture at the University of Cape Town and former director of the Constitution of Public Intellectual Life Research Project. She has published widely, including her book *Terrific Majesty: The Powers of Shaka Zulu and the Limits of Historical Invention.*

George Hartley is associate professor of English at Ohio University, where he teaches decolonization theories and literatures. He is the author of *Textual Politics and the Language Poets* (Indiana University Press, 1989) and *The Abyss of Representation: Marxism and the Postmodern Sublime* (Duke University Press, 2003). Currently Hartley is working on a book manuscript titled "The Curandera of Conquest: Gloria Anzaldúa's Decolonizing Consciousness."

Janet Hess is an associate professor of art history in the Hutchins School of Liberal Studies at Sonoma State University. She is the author of *Art and Architecture in Postcolonial Africa* (2006), as well as numerous articles on postcolonial art, architecture, and representations of the body. She received her JD from the University of Iowa, her MA in art history from Columbia University, and her PhD from Harvard University.

T. Spreelin (Spree) MacDonald is a visiting assistant professor of English and African Studies at Ohio University. His research primarily concerns South African literature, oral and written, as well as critical race theory and South African intellectual history. He has articles published and forthcoming on the works of Vonani Bila and the Timbila Poetry Project, Zakes Mda, Kopano Matlwa, Lesego Rampolokeng, and Phaswane Mpe, among others.

Ebenezer Adebisi Olawuyi teaches in the Department of Communication and Language Arts at the University of Ibadan in Nigeria. His research agenda is on international communication, media, and cultural studies, with particular interest in evolving an African media system that would respond to the peculiar development challenge of the continent. He belongs to several academic and professional associations, including African Council for Communication Education (ACCE), International Reading Association (IRA), American Studies Association of Nigeria (ASAN), Nigerian Institute of Public Relations (NIPR), and Pan African Media Research Organization (PAMRO). He is also a laureate of the Council for the Development of Social Science Research in Africa (CODESRIA).

Steve Odero Ouma holds a bachelor's of law (LLB) degree from the University of Nairobi in Kenya, and a master's in human rights and democratization in Africa (LLM) from the University of Pretoria in South Africa (2005). He is currently a PhD candidate in political theory at Luiss University of Rome in Italy.

Oyèrónké̩ é̩ Oyĕwùmí was born in Nigeria and educated at the University of Ibadan and the University of California at Berkeley. Oyĕwùmí has been widely recognized for her work. Her monograph *The Invention of Women: Making an African Sense of Western Gender Discourses* won the 1998 Distinguished Book Award of the American Sociological Association, and was a finalist for the Herskovits Prize of the African Studies Association in the same year. She has garnered a number of research fellowships, including Rockefeller fellowships, a presidential fellowship, and a Ford Foundation grant. She is the editor of *African Gender Studies: Conceptual Issues / Theoretical Questions*, as well as *African Women and Feminism: Reflecting on the Politics of Sisterhood.*

Tsenay Serequeberhan received his PhD in philosophy from Boston College in 1988. Eritrean by birth, he is a professor of philosophy at Morgan State University, whose work is grounded in the Continental tradition and focused on African/Africana philosophy and social-political philosophy. His research explores the intersection of these areas of scholarly concern. He is the author of *African Philosophy: The Essential Readings* (1991); *The Hermeneutics of African Philosophy* (1994); *Our Heritage* (2000); and *Contested Memory* (2007). He is presently working on a book to be titled *Existence and Heritage.*

Index

Achebe, Chinua, 43, 145
Adichie, Chimamanda, 37, 38, 39, 41, 42, 43, 44, 47, 51, 52, 58, 61, 62, 63
aesthetics, 160, 172
Africa,
    and colonial interests, 104
    and colonialism, 103, 104
    journalistic traditions in, 103
    media systems in, 103, 104, 105
    and Western ideology, 105
    and Western media, 105
African Americans, 15, 16, 18, 19, 21, 22, 23, 24
African art, 160, 161, 162, 163, 164, 165, 166, 173
African art history, 160, 162, 163, 165–66, 174
African Broadcasting Network, 128
African media operations, 108
    normative theory of, 108–9, 110
African National Congress (ANC), 84, 86, 87, 89, 90, 92, 93, 95, 96
African Renaissance, 117, 119, 120, 126, 127, 128
African socialism, 16
African Social Reality, 111
African Union/Organization of African

Unity, 118
agenda-setter/setting, 86, 89
Age of Enlightenment, 144
Al-Jazeera, 129, 130
Ansu-Kyeremeh, Kwasi, 111
apartheid, 69, 70, 72, 73, 104
A24, 129

Biafra, 37, 38, 41, 43, 52, 55, 56, 57, 58, 59, 60, 62, 63
Biko, Steve, 69, 70, 71, 72, 73, 74, 75, 76, 77, 79
Bila, Vonani, 69, 77, 78, 79
Black Consciousness, 69, 70, 71, 72, 74, 75, 76, 77, 79
body/bodies, 28, 30, 31, 32

Cabral, Amilcar, 1, 6, 150
Castoriadis, Cornelius, 157
Cesaire, Aime, 4–5, 51
Chipkin, Ivor, 87
citizenship, 83, 85, 93, 94, 95, 97
civil rights movement (U.S.), 16
colonialism, 90, 91, 94, 95, 97, 104
colonial residue, 146
Congo (Democratic Republic of), 16, 17, 18, 19, 20

contemporary inheritance, 146
counterpublic, 91

Davidson, Basil, 142
debate, 83, 84, 85, 86, 87, 91, 92, 94, 95, 96, 97
decolonization, 137
detraumatization, 38, 41, 62, 63
double game, 145
double traumatization, 37, 38, 39, 41, 42

emergence, 69, 74, 75, 76
Enlightenment, 83, 84, 89, 94, 95, 97
Eze, Emmanuel, 2

Fanon, Frantz, 1, 41, 44, 53, 143, 146
Fraser, Nancy, 91, 96

Gadamer, Hans-Georg, 147
gatekeepers, 84, 96
Geldoff, Bob, 122
gender, 29, 160, 161, 162, 164, 165, 166, 168
gendercentric/ism, 160, 169
genderism/ist, 160, 161, 165, 166
globalization, 107
global mediascape, 106
Gordon, Lewis, 2
Gramsci, Antonio, 83, 89

Habermas, Jürgen, 83, 96
Hegel, G. W. F., 139
Hyland, Drew A., 152

imperialism, 104
indigenous knowledge, 37, 38, 39, 45, 47, 49, 51, 52, 54, 55, 60, 61, 62, 63, 162
intellectual(s), 83, 84, 85, 86, 87, 88, 89, 90, 91, 93, 95, 96, 97, 98

journalism, 84, 93, 95

Kafka's ape, 143
Kant, Immanuel, 83, 139

Kaunda, Kenneth, 103
Kenya, 15, 17
Kenyatta, Jomo, 15, 16

literature, 69, 72, 74, 75, 77, 79
Lumumba, Patrice, 15, 20, 27, 28, 31, 32, 33, 34, 35

MacBride Commission, 107
Malcolm X, 15–26
Mangcu, Xolela, 97
Marcuse, Herbert, 150
masculinity, 27, 28, 29, 31, 32, 34
Mau Mau, 15, 17, 26
Mbeki, Thabo, 86, 87, 88, 89, 92, 120
Mda, Zakes, 69, 75, 76
media, 84, 85, 86, 89, 90, 91, 92, 93, 94, 95, 96, 102
 as fourth estate, 102
 watchdog function of, 105
Memmi, Albert, 144
metaphysical anchoring-stones, 145
metaphysical tradition, 137
Mississippi, 15, 16, 22, 26
mixed heritage/hybrid heritage, 150
Moemeka, Andrew, 111
motherhood, 160, 162, 169–72, 174

nationalism, 29, 30, 31, 37, 38, 47, 51
Native Club, 90, 91
Ndebele, Njabulo, 69, 72, 73, 74, 75, 76, 77, 78
NEPAD, 120
Nietzsche, Friedrich, 138
Nigeria, 37, 38, 39, 40, 41, 42, 43, 44, 45, 46, 47, 51, 52, 54, 55, 56, 58, 59, 60, 61, 62, 63
Nkrumah, Kwame, 27, 28, 29, 30, 31, 34, 35
Nyerere, Julius, 27, 28, 143, 144

Obeng-Quaidoo, Isaac, 111
Okigbo, Charles, 111
orchestration/orchestrating, 94, 96

Ousmane, Sembène, 146
Oyewumi, Oyeronke, 2–3

paradigm shift, 140
Pate, Umar, 110
postapartheid, 69, 75, 76, 124
post-traumatic stress disorder (PTSD),
    38, 40, 44, 63
public interest, 84, 90, 92, 93, 94, 95, 97
public opinion, 89, 90
public sphere, 83, 85, 89, 91, 97

race/racial/racialize/racism, 85, 87, 88,
    90, 91, 95, 97
Rampolokeng, Lesego, 69, 75, 76, 77, 78
reason(ing), 83, 89, 94
rediscovery, 74, 75
Rousseau, Jacques, 148

Said, Edward W., 83, 141, 149
Saro-Wiwa, Ken, 6
Seepe, Sipho, 87, 88, 89, 97
self, 69, 70, 71, 72, 73, 74, 75, 76, 77, 79
Senghor, Léopold Sédar, 143, 144
slavery, 26, 104
South Africa, 3, 23, 69, 70, 72, 73, 75, 76,
    77, 84, 85, 86, 89, 90, 91, 92, 93, 97,
    98, 124

South African Broadcasting Corporation
    (SABC), 86, 92, 93, 95, 129
spectacle, 69, 72, 73, 74, 75, 76
symmetry of images, 147

testimonio (witness) literature, 37, 39
Thiong'o, Ngugi wa, 2, 6, 48
trauma, 37, 38, 39, 40, 41, 44, 47, 57, 58
Truth and Reconciliation Commission
    (TRC), 85, 86
Tutu, Desmond, 89

United States, 16, 19, 21, 25
University of Maiduguri, 110

Vattimo, Gianni, 137, 145

Warner, Michael, 96
Western media, 104–6, 118, 121, 122,
    127, 130
    and African media, 105–13
    and misrepresentation, 108
Westernized African, 142
worldsense, 162

Yoruba, 160–74